sweet alchemy

YIGIT PURA

sweet alchemy

dessert magic

WITH SEANA WEAVER

PHOTOGRAPHS BY FRANKIE FRANKENY

CHRONICLE BOOKS

SAN FRANCISCO

sweet alchemy is dedicated to my friend Sherry Yard.

By kismet, sometimes the universe brings a person into our lives,
and we can't remember the time before we came to know such a soul.

Your kindness and generosity of spirit is rare in this world, and I'm grateful
to call you my friend.

You are my alchemist.

xo

Library of Congress Cataloging-in-Publication Data available.
ISBN 978-1-4521-0888-9

Manufactured in China

FSC
www.fsc.org
MIX
Paper from
responsible sources
FSC® C104723

Designed by **ANNE KENADY**
Prop and food styling by **YIGIT PURA**
Thank you to Gump's for providing beautiful tableware for our photo shoot.

10 9 8 7 6 5 4 3 2 1

Chronicle Books LLC
680 Second Street
San Francisco, California 94107
www.chroniclebooks.com

acknowledgments

Since the age of five, when I started digging around my mom's kitchen cabinets, this culinary journey has been made even sweeter thanks to some wonderful souls in my life. . . .

Seana Weaver, for co-authoring this book with me, and helping *Sweet Alchemy* take life.

Sebnem, for always being my number-one champion! Super friend for life!

Frankie Frankeny, for not only having patience in understanding my vision in this book but also bringing it to life with such gorgeous photography!

Dad, thanks for pushing me to pursue my dreams.

My dog, Maui, for being the best sidekick a chef could ever want. Thanks for being so perky at 3:00 A.M., and for the endless snuggles and that one-of-a-kind smile!

My best friend, Ken, for pushing me forward, and having the patience to keep pushing me forward.

My partners, MeMe and Janet, for being crazy enough to say, "Do you want to make Tout Sweet happen?" I am so grateful to have you two on my team.

My team at Tout Sweet, who believe in my crazy vision and support me in every way they can, especially Jessica Rohrig for always being such a trouper. Thank you from the bottom of my heart.

Björk and *Le Petit Prince* for being a generous source of warmth and inspiration.

My mom, Handi, for letting me lick the bottom of the mixing bowl when I was a kid.

My mentors, Joanna Karlinsky, Luis Robledo-Richards, Eric Bertoia, Mark Fiorentino, and Daniel Boulud, for not only teaching me technique but also shaping me into a professional, and harnessing my crazy energy in my twenties.

All the farmers who work tirelessly to provide me with the best produce this chef could hope for!

San Francisco, I will always love you lustfully. Couldn't ask for a better home.

Dan Strone at Trident Media and the entire team at Chronicle Books.

My agent and friend Deb Goldfarb . . . and to the marathon.

And most sincerely to all of our sweet followers at Tout Sweet. Seeing your eyes light up with joy as you eat dessert is the single biggest pleasure of this chef's life.

xo

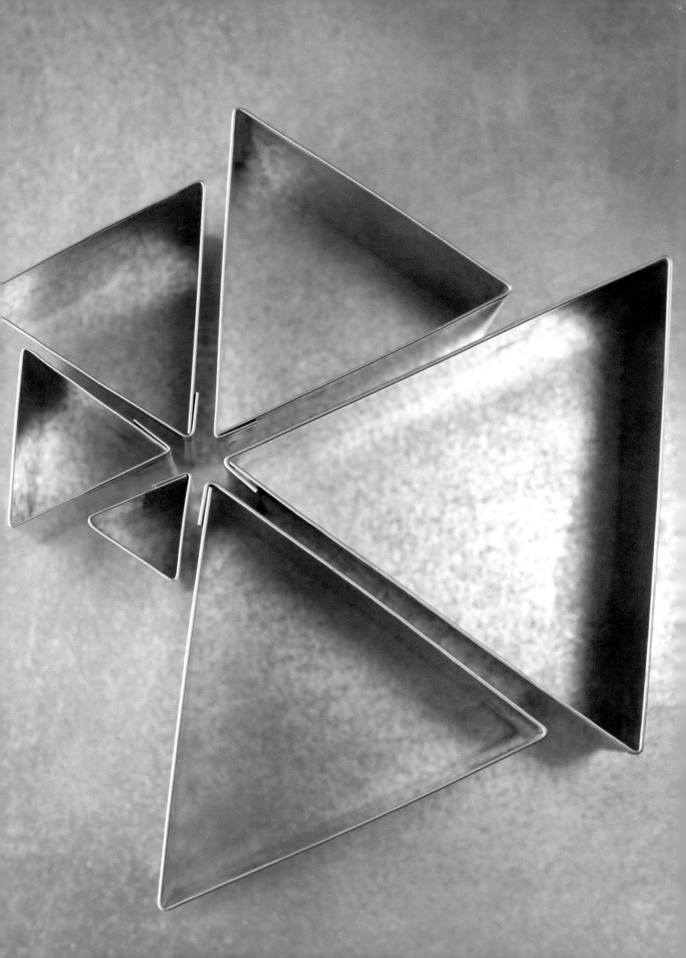

"If you want to build a ship, don't gather people together to collect wood and don't assign them tasks and work, but rather, teach them to long for the endless immensity of the sea." —ANTOINE DE SAINT-EXUPÉRY

introduction

You see, it all began with a spoonful of burnt sugar. At five years old, I was giddy with anticipation every time my mother made crème caramel. I would hang around the kitchen, smelling and yearning while my mother mixed and measured.

To make a crème caramel, you have to burn some sugar in a pan to a dark amber color, until it reaches the perfect balance of sweet and bitter. This caramel is poured into ramekins and topped with a creamy custard. Most people will then dunk their warm pan, caramel clinging to its bottom, into hot water to clean it. Not my mother. She's a clever woman. She'd take a spoon and swirl up all the remaining caramel, let it harden on the spoon, and then hand it to me. It was the perfect way to cork a talkative kid. My first favorite candy was this caramel spoon, made by the first chef I ever knew: my *anne*, or mother.

I was born with what my family refers to as "The Little Prince syndrome." I

questioned everything in the world, and *why* was—and may still be—my favorite and most oft-repeated word. My mom longed for a quiet hour or two every week, and the caramel spoonful was the way she found it. I licked my sweet pacifier for hours, happy and quiet, allowing my mother some peace.

Flash forward a few decades, and crème caramel is still one of my favorite simple pleasures, with its complex, sweet-bitter flavor and luscious texture. Most of all, it tastes of nostalgia. I shocked friends recently at a birthday party where the host's Mexican mother served three huge dishes of crème caramel. I helped myself to five servings.

It wasn't just this magic spoon that made me fall in love with sweets and desserts. Growing up in Turkey, I was spoiled with great pastry from a very young age. Turkish pâtisseries carried everything from traditional Turkish desserts, including buttery sweet baklava, to French éclairs and strawberry fraisier cakes. In Turkey, you don't need a special occasion to eat cake. We believe life is in the living, especially with the people you cherish, so what better way to celebrate every day than with a wonderful dessert at the end of a meal?

I've always felt blessed to have found my passion as a pastry chef, especially given the setbacks I encountered early on. When I was young, due to cultural stereotypes, I was discouraged from being in the kitchen because I was a boy. But where there's love, there is a way. I practically stumbled upon my first restaurant job at the age of twenty. From there I serendipitously carved my path in a profession that has always challenged and rewarded me through beauty and pleasure.

As a Buddhist, I believe the path to enlightenment is in striving to find the middle ground between all extremes. I try to hear, feel, and see all extremes simultaneously and to create harmony from these opposites. For me, envisioning and creating desserts is no different. Ask anyone who knows me well, and they will tell you that I have a crazy, and at times uncontained, level of energy in life and in the kitchen. I never create a new dish thinking, "I should make a tart," or "I want to create a new cake." I first draw from memories of flavors; like a librarian, every time I smell or taste something, I try to categorize it in a file in my brain. When it is time to create, I draw from these files of memories and think of how to pair flavors together in harmony. I especially love pairing things that are complete opposites in flavor, and at times harsh by themselves, to create a harmonious

flavor profile on the palate. Then I think about what sort of emotion and feeling that dessert should evoke; I want the dessert to have a personality of its own. And at last, I draw from my memory of inspirations and history to give it identity and form.

In dessert creation, I pull from more than just taste and smell memories. Flashes of an exhibit I saw at the Pompidou in Paris, in which I was fascinated by an architect's use of angles and light to create dimensions and space, will lead to a plate design. The memory of a sweet sakura mochi from a small bakery in New York City, eaten during the winter, inspires me to create an ice cream flavor. Coming forward when I need a different citrus flavor will be the scent of the kumquat peel that I scratched and sniffed at the farmers' market a few days ago. I experience and am inspired by a new obsession with cashew and black sesame praline while Miles Davis plays in our kitchen at Tout Sweet. It's an organized chaos of sorts. I'm lucky to have found pastry as my source of inspiration, as well as daily practice in meditation, trying to find harmony every day. I aim to piece together my love of food and flavors with sentiments and emotions, with surges of inspiration to create unique desserts, which I hope linger in people's memories long after they eat them. This is what I live for as a chef. If I can achieve this on a genuine level 5 percent of the time, I will be most grateful. The other 95 percent is hard work. This process, and more so the love of this process, is sweet alchemy to me.

I've been curious as to why home cooks are so intimidated by dessert, especially when it's the course people get most excited about. Is it the science? The technique? Or all the myths that have been built around it for decades, such as the mythically temperamental soufflé? I would like to break these boundaries and build bridges to all the brave and soulful home chefs who bake their sweet hearts out!

In each chapter of this book, I introduce the reader to one of the basic ingredients of dessert, and to fundamental recipes, creating a unique way to approach the creation of desserts. Harnessing the knowledge of how to work with simple ingredients is the basic template for what I call "sweet alchemy." First I explore the ingredient, and then I introduce the simple science of composition. Finally I introduce technique, beginning with simple recipes and progressing to more complex ones. I hope your curiosity will be sparked and you will be infected with my pure love of the process and its sweet results.

A final note: Here in San Francisco we have a very simple approach to food— eat local and sustainable, buy organic when you can, and, most important, cook with love. I have learned to marry my European training with my Californian sensibilities and in the process have fallen in love with my new hometown. Working with fresh, local ingredients is one of the best ways to quickly improve your baking. Whenever possible, I recommend using local, organic ingredients; these recipes should be a good way to do that.

I humbly invite you to experience the beauty of food and desserts in a most organic manner, and to be inspired in the process.

harnessing alchemy

Alchemy is the bringing together of two different, unrelated elements to create a third, greater element. In ancient times, the alchemist sought ways to turn lead into gold or water into a life-extending elixir. I look every day to find the perfect confluence of my ingredients so that sweet gold might come out of my kitchen. What I call "sweet alchemy" is the melding of three components—the chef's culinary heritage, the chef's personal interpretation of a dish, and the technique and science of creation—to create something spectacular.

Respecting the heritage of food is very important to me. Foods of different countries are directly influenced by their culture and their heritage and therefore have a distinct story. And often each dish has a unique historical context that makes it special. It is important to understand this, in each and every dish. As a modern chef, I really enjoy putting my personal touch on classic recipes, but I always want to make sure they retain their original voices. When making a tarte Tatin (which may be one of my top five favorite desserts of all time), I like to play with subtle flavors of spices and honey, but I want to make sure that the Tatin sisters who originally created this dish would still be proud of it.

• • •

When I was beginning my career, my culinary school experience was cut short for financial reasons. At the time, it felt like the world's greatest heartbreak and a huge setback. In retrospect, it is clear to me that it was a defining moment. In order to learn, I was forced to apprentice in kitchens and learn directly from chefs as they worked. Stepping away from traditional school meant that I had a singular culinary adventure. To this day, I tell aspiring cooks to apprentice as much as possible. Each chef lends his or her culinary heritage to the craft in unique ways, and the best thing for young cooks to do is to soak up each drop of knowledge and later on sift through those experiences, take the best of them, and create their own philosophy of food.

My career has been shaped and pushed by the great chefs that I have had the honor to apprentice with and am now able to call my colleagues. I will never forget the day when I first walked into the kitchen of Le Cirque 2000 in New York City, where I met my true pastry mentor, Luis Robledo-Richards. I recall thinking, "If there is a heaven, this must be it." I was determined to learn everything I could from this master chocolatier. Daily, I showed up for work three to four hours early and completed my prep list long before my shift was over. I would then find the chef and follow him around, asking questions about his chocolate work. Each day I would follow and ask, and each day Chef Robledo-Richards would shoo me away and refuse to answer my questions. After weeks of this dance, just when I had resigned myself to learning by watching, he decided that I wasn't going to give up. He took me under his wing, and so my chocolate training began. It was through this persistence that I learned how to temper and work with chocolate, craft multitiered cakes, and so on.

But if I learned technique from Luis, I learned the true love and respect of food from Daniel Boulud. At the age of twenty-four, I took on the position of pastry sous-chef at Daniel (Daniel Boulud's four-star restaurant). Looking back, I see that this was simply crazy. Working in this kitchen, and leading a team of fourteen people, really made me the chef that I am today. Over the course of two and a half years, I had the honor of working with boulanger Mark Fiorentino, as well as pastry chefs Eric Bertoia and my friend Dominique Ansel. Working with these three creative minds, I started to develop concepts of my own, and for the first time I came to see my own mad-scientist creations come to life. But it was while working under Daniel Boulud that I learned to respect food, its history and heritage, and the process of creating new dishes: carefully considering each flavor and texture and selecting the right ingredients to create harmony. Most of all, I recall how Daniel would always try a new dish from the standpoint of the client, considering what their thought process would be, to ensure the highest standard in satisfaction.

• • •

Today, I look for the same hunger, drive, and ambition in the young cooks who come into my kitchen. It is not enough that they demonstrate intelligence and the ability to remember and recite ratios and the temperature of boiling sugar. I look for passion, love, and excitement in their eyes and in their actions, in the way they approach their job every day, willing to do simple, repetitive tasks but with the constant curiosity to create and develop new ideas. I am excited and willing to empty the contents of my brain into their

hands, but I need to see this drive first. Someone recently asked me if I have my cooks sign confidentiality agreements when they begin in my kitchen. This is beyond my scope of understanding. Culinary heritage is based on a long line of chefs and cooks who have openly shared their recipes and techniques with new generations. I have no interest in being the end of that tradition. I don't write down the entire procedures, but I hope that these young people will take what they learn from me, my sous chef, and their colleagues and carry it forward to the next generation of pâtisseries. And here in this book, I give some of my recipes, and hopefully some of my experiences, to you.

Each dessert, pastry, or sweet has its own culinary legacy. Many breads date back hundreds of years, some having been developed through painstaking trial and error and others coming out of happy accidents or the necessity of the time. Around the holidays, I make a bûche de Noël, or yule log. An homage to the warming hearth and burning log that has been baked and shaped for more than a hundred years, it is one of the most recognizably traditional cakes that we serve at my bakery, Tout Sweet. Understanding a dessert's heritage is crucial to creating a well-founded version of it. Alchemy begins when a chef understands the dessert's heritage and his or her own relationship with the dessert. My bûche is made with a chocolate génoise cake and a coffee buttercream frosting. Recently, I had to take a business trip to Chicago just as the holiday season was getting under way—to step away from my kitchen at that time of year was nerve-racking! I didn't have time to train a cook to make the bûche before I left for the weekend trip, and so I filled the cooler with an overstock. Imagine my surprise when I returned to a restocked cooler of the cakes. The kitchen did run out of original stock, but an enterprising cook had been watching me and taking notes. He stepped in while I was gone and made sure the store had enough to sell. I consider this a giant success in my kitchen—a young cook who had the foresight and intelligence to watch and learn. When it came time to step in, he did so with grace and gusto. As a chef, nothing makes me prouder than seeing a young talent working under me develop not only the skill level but also the confidence to lead a kitchen, and take some of the weight off of my shoulders.

It takes practice to be able to perfect a technique. The only way to learn most pastry techniques is to be willing to mess up over and over again. Understanding the science always helps—and in my opinion, it is necessary. Knowing why and how things happen in cooking means that you will be much less likely to skip a step and more likely to reproduce the sweet correctly each time.

• • •

The good things in life often take a lot of time and reflection, and pastry is no different. It is an exacting science. A lot of repetition occurs in a professional kitchen to make sure two people make the same recipe in exactly the same way. Small details can affect the outcome of the final product significantly. I cannot stress enough how important it is to really follow and understand each process and the use of each ingredient, whether it is one that adds flavor or one that affects the texture of the dish.

The mark of a great baker is that the food appears to be effortless. Underneath this appearance, however, is the appreciation of organization, and strict attention to method. We take flavors and ingredients gathered from nature, sift them through our knowledge of preparation and technique, and mold them with our creativity and curiosity to create delicious dishes. This trifecta of gathering, formulating, and creating is the continual process that drives every great baker.

understanding your workshop: tools

This section gives basic guidelines regarding measurements, equipment, ingredients, and methods. These are the day-to-day tools of the pastry kitchen, and you'll want to be familiar with them as we get into the recipes in this book. I also think of this as a second round of acknowledgments. Although there are many people in my life who have helped me get to where I am, I would be lost without my tool kit.

it's all in the details:
mise en place, be prepared!

Mise en place is a French phrase that translates to "put in place." This was one of the first terms I heard in the kitchen when I started as a pantry cook, and though at the time I didn't immediately grasp its importance, it's a mantra I've come to live by as a professional chef. It refers to a sense of organization and readiness, in which you know where everything you need is when you need it, at every step of the cooking process.

I always tell my cooks to have all their tools ready and all their ingredients measured prior to starting each task.

You will find this very helpful at home as well. In making desserts and baking, it is nearly impossible to stop halfway through the process to run out to the store for an ingredient; in more temperamental recipes, spending 2 minutes to take out the flour, measure it, and sift it will bring ruin. Being well prepared in advance allows you the peace of mind to focus on the task at hand and to put love into the process, and it will improve your final product immeasurably.

the basics

DIGITAL SCALE. Let me state firmly here that grams are a baker's best friend. I cannot stress this strongly enough. I know that most kitchens and cookbooks refer to cups, tablespoons, and other measurements, but grams are the easiest form of measuring ingredients accurately and simply. In every professional kitchen I've worked, we've measured everything in grams on a digital scale, be it flour, chocolate, milk, or eggs. With a scale, you don't have to go back and forth between different cumbersome measuring tools, and therefore you can work quickly and efficiently. But most important, you will get the same yield every single time. With volume measurements such as cups, there is always room for human error. One person's level cup measure may not be the same as the next person's. But 100 grams of flour will always be just that. Another big advantage of working with a scale is that you can keep measuring things on top of one another in the same bowl, without having to dirty an entire set of measuring cups. Just use the tare/zero button or your math skills.

With eggs, I always weigh them out of the shell. An egg white is estimated at 30 g and an egg yolk is estimated at 20 g.

OFFSET SPATULA. Alongside a Sharpie marker in my chef's coat pocket, there is always a small offset spatula. This is an extremely versatile tool, used for smoothing out filling and ganache, as well as lifting cakes and breads from baking sheets. Putting together most desserts becomes easier and more enjoyable with the use of it, and the offset spatula is my favorite tool in the kitchen.

RUBBER SPATULA. With the advent of silicone, rubber spatulas have become almost universally heat-resistant. I encourage you to always check the packaging, because losing a pan of milk to a melted-rubber surprise is a kitchen heartbreak that can be easily avoided. A heat-resistant rubber spatula is extremely useful for cooking milk-based custards and melting chocolates.

WHISK. The whisk is a basic, indispensable kitchen tool. Don't fall into the trap of buying fancy silicone-coated whisks; just stick with the basic stainless-steel model. A whisk is a simple and easy way to add air into a fatty liquid or to ensure that dry ingredients are well combined. I always have at least three sizes on hand: small, medium, and balloon. The balloon is wonderful for hand-whisking meringues and chantilly cream. If you already hand-whisk sometimes, this tool will make you feel as though you're cheating!

FINE-MESH STRAINER. I call for a strainer in several recipes. A good, sturdy fine-mesh strainer will improve your kitchen tool kit immeasurably. Whether used for straining a consommé or pastry cream, a really good mesh strainer will allow you to produce a smooth and clear product without any lumps or undesired pieces. Be sure that you have a large bowl that it fits in.

THERMOMETER. I am going to say this once and be done with it: Candy thermometers don't work. They have to be fitted to the pot in a way that forces you to put your face in extremely hot steam in order to read them, and one that is fitted correctly is going to take the temperature of only one part of the pot. Don't bother. Here's my solution: Use a long-stemmed, digital instant-read thermometer. You can put it into the cooking liquid at different places and at different levels, giving you a better overall temperature reading. For cooking sugar and tempering chocolate, a thermometer is absolutely necessary.

PARCHMENT PAPER (THICK). I would be lost without parchment paper. In my kitchens, we always use the thickest brand we can find. A thicker paper stands up to our abuse and stays flat during baking. My biggest tip for parchment paper: Don't skip it. If I call for it, what you're baking will stick to a bare pan. You can almost always replace parchment paper with a Silpat (a silicone lining for a baking sheet), which is a lot less wasteful but adds to your cleanup.

BAIN-MARIE. Also called a double boiler, this arrangement of bowls and pots creates a simple dispersion of direct heat, forcing it through water and into steam to heat things gently and indirectly. A double boiler will keep chocolate from burning and will cook fruit at a slow, even pace. You can buy a contraption sold as a bain-marie, but I'm certain that you already have the elements of one in your kitchen. A medium saucepan fitted with a glass or stainless-steel bowl on top (or even another, smaller saucepan) will do the trick. Remember that this is a gentle cooking method, so the water should be at a simmer, not a boil. The edge of the bowl, where it comes into contact with the saucepan, will be very hot, and that will be where the contents are most likely to stick or burn, so use a rubber spatula to move things away from that area. Legend has it that the bain-marie

was an essential tool for alchemy. In fact, the Marie that the name refers to was possibly one of the first alchemists, making it a perfect tool for sweet alchemy.

HANDHELD BLENDER. If you don't already have one, get one! A sturdy handheld or immersion blender will emulsify your chocolate, whip your custard into silky loveliness, and incorporate butter into any creamy delight.

SALT. In more ways than one, salt is a tool in any kitchen. Like sugar, it pulls out water from most natural ingredients during cooking, so adding a touch of it to fruits during cooking will help them to soften up. I always use kosher salt as my basic salt—never table salt. With kosher salt, there are few, if any, additives, so you know what you're getting. Table salt is usually iodized and can alter the taste of a dish. Many of my recipes include Maldon sea salt or fleur de sel. Both are made up of very large flakes and should be used sparingly. You'll find that using flake salts as an ingredient or sprinkled on a dish just before serving will increase the potency of all the flavors of the dish and make eating it more of an experience.

SUGAR

cooking sugar [26]

lavender honey agar-agar gems [28]

burnt caramel sauce [30]

butterscotch sauce [32]

honey molasses candied almonds [33]

pistachio—vietnamese cinnamon brittle [34]

hazelnut spears [37]

We begin our love of desserts with sugar, the key ingredient to all things sweet. Sugar has a bad reputation nowadays. I've been a fan of sweets since I was a young boy, and to this day I eat a ton of sugar.

It's all about finding a happy balance in your overall diet. As in Buddhism, being in harmony is a matter of finding a happy medium between two opposites. In my kitchen at Tout Sweet, it's no secret that during the day I live on sugar and caffeine. I never hold myself back from having a warm scone fresh out of the oven, or a piece of chocolate cake as one of my chefs cuts it. But in the latter part of my day I counterbalance this by exercising when I can, and I always take care to have a healthful dinner.

I literally wear "sugar" on my body for the world to see. When I was twenty-four years old and was hired at Daniel in New York City as the pastry sous chef, I couldn't have been more excited and nervous. I knew this was a big responsibility at such a young age, and it would come with many challenges, but I had a hunger to learn everything I could about desserts. It was love. In order to never forget my love for dessert, I got the compound formula for sucrose ($H_{12}C_{22}O_{11}$) tattooed on the bottom of my neck. Sugar and I are married for life, which is appropriate since it is my first love in the world.

Sugar is to desserts as salt is to savory food: a flavor enhancer. It shouldn't be the prominent flavor. If your first thought after tasting a dessert is, "It's very sweet," that's not a good sign. When used in the right balance, sugar can make the bitter-sweetness of chocolate bolder, brighten citrus, make berries more robust and stone fruit more sultry, and bring a melody to custards and sauces.

Like salt, sugar can act as a preservative. Jams and preserves are usually 80 percent sugar and 20 percent fruit. This helps preserve the fruit, extending its shelf life. An opened jar of jam can sit at room temperature for months without going bad. Adding sugar is also a great way to preserve fruits in the freezer. Weighing your fruit and adding 10 percent of its weight in sugar before puréeing it to freeze will help prevent crystallization and will protect the flavor. Given the cost of quality fruit, this is a great way to save money when you have extra. Sometimes I get greedy—I have a hard time saying good-bye to flavors as the seasons pass—so I buy very ripe fruits at the farmers' market, purée them, and keep them in my freezer. That way I can have access to these flavors year-round.

• • •

In my pastry pantry, "sugar" refers to more than just granulated white sugar.

Different sugars and sweeteners have their own characters in their flavors, the way they cook through different stages, and the textures they create in different desserts. It's important to be familiar with different sweeteners, not only to understand how to substitute one for the other, but also to understand how they can affect the outcome of your creations. The following are some of the common and uncommon sugars and sweeteners I use.

AGAVE NECTAR is a sweet syrup usually found in the sugar aisle and is made from the same cactus as tequila—can't complain about that. It does taste sweeter than granulated white sugar, so I recommend using a bit less of it if you substitute it for sugar. Unlike honey or other inverted sugars, agave nectar doesn't tend to seize up when cold and will easily dissolve when stirred into a liquid. This makes it a good sweetener for cocktails and other cold drinks or preparations. Its flavor is very neutral, and I find that it brings a bit of sweet without much depth when added to recipes.

BROWN SUGAR has a distinctive brown color due to the presence of molasses. It is either an unrefined or partially refined soft sugar consisting of sugar crystals with some residual molasses content, or a refined white sugar to which molasses has been added. Depending on the type, brown sugars can contain anywhere from 3.5 to 10 percent molasses, giving them a deeper bitter flavor as well as making them more hydroscopic, or moist. It's important to keep this quality in mind when thinking of substituting brown sugar in certain recipes, as it will affect not only the flavor but also the texture of your desserts.

CORN SYRUP is a sweet syrup made from the starches of corn. It is essential in some recipes, not only for flavor but also because its viscosity acts as a thickener. Corn syrup is an invert sugar, which helps to prevent crystallization in cooked sugar products. This is what helps a ganache keep its glistening silkiness.

GLUCOSE SYRUP, which is most commonly used in professional pastry kitchens, has properties similar to those of corn syrup. It is made primarily from starches such as wheat, potatoes, and tapioca. In most recipes, glucose syrup and corn syrup are interchangeable.

HONEY is a topic I could write an entire book about. It is a sweet food made by bees, using the nectar from flowers. It is about 20 percent sweeter than regular sugar, which is good to keep in mind when substituting honey for sugar in recipes. Its moist viscosity also helps to impart a unique character to desserts and baked goods. Honey is nature's natural invert sugar. It not only helps prevent premature crystallization, but also can help prevent drying in certain recipes by naturally absorbing humidity from the environment. Honey is a wonderful natural antihistamine, and eating some local honey every day is a great way to suppress seasonal pollen allergies.

Honey can have a variety of flavor profiles, depending on the source of the nectar, and is classified by its floral source. Its delicate flavors have inspired me in numerous desserts throughout the seasons. I urge you to try different kinds of honey from farmers' markets and local stores. Some of my favorites include lavender, star thistle, orange blossom, and wildflower.

MAPLE SYRUP is a traditional North American sweetener, prepared from the sap of the sugar maple tree. It has a dark amber color and a deep, rich flavor that is unique. It's not as sweet as honey nor as bitter as molasses, and it has a natural, earthy quality to it. I think this makes it a wonderful component to most fall and winter desserts. When purchasing maple syrup, read the label to verify that it is real maple syrup. Most maple-type syrups in the United States are in fact corn syrup that has had caramel coloring added. Maple sugar is what remains after maple syrup is cooked until all the liquid has boiled away. Visually it resembles a much lighter brown sugar. Its flavor is very delicate. Maple sugar isn't as moist as brown sugar, making it easier to substitute for white sugar in certain recipes. I've played with using maple sugar as a whole or partial substitution in recipes that require a cooked sugar, such as meringue, Chiboust, or parfait.

MOLASSES is a viscous by-product of the processing of sugarcane, grapes, or sugar beets into sugar. The quality of a molasses depends on the maturity of the cane, grapes, or beets. I find that, when used very minimally, molasses can add a unique depth to certain desserts that may normally fall flat.

MUSCOVADO SUGAR, also known as Barbados sugar, is an unrefined sugar with a strong molasses flavor. If available, I prefer it to brown sugar in some recipes, as it has a more mature flavor profile without being overly sweet. It pairs beautifully with coffee, spices, and foods with bold flavors. It isn't cheap, but it is certainly worth exploring.

PALM SUGAR was originally made from the sugary sap of date palms; however, these days it's mainly produced from the sap of coconut palms. It's quickly gaining popularity in the health community over agave nectar. The taste of pure coconut palm sugar is really brilliant. It resembles brown sugar, with a much more delicate body and rounded caramel and butterscotch notes. Palm sugar's low melting point and high burn temperature make it suitable for confections and candies.

RAW SUGARS comprise yellow to brown sugars made by clarifying the source syrup with heat until it becomes a crystalline solid, retaining a deeper flavor. Sugar in the Raw and turbinado sugar are the most commonly known raw sugars.

WHITE SUGAR, also known as sucrose, is essentially raw crystallized sugar. The sugarcane goes through a process of extraction during which the molasses is removed to give it a pure, sweet flavor. It is then further processed to remove other flavors and colors, resulting in the granulated white sugar that we know and love. White sugar is produced from either sugarcane or sugar beets. Production of sugar from sugar beets is considerably cheaper, but I always buy sugar made from sugarcane, as it tends to have the purest flavor.

COOKING SUGAR

Sugar is fascinating. When cooked directly, it goes through a range of different stages and moods, allowing us to manipulate form, texture, and flavor in the final dessert. You may have heard terms like *soft ball*, *hard ball*, and *hard crack*. These refer to the state of sugar when it's cooked to certain temperatures, not to a type of extreme sport.

I am obsessed with numbers and ratios, because they never lie. When cooking sugar to the hard ball stage, many chefs will pull a spoonful from the cooking sugar and dip it in cool water. If the sugar seizes and becomes hard, it is considered done. I don't like this method because it leaves too much to chance and means that you have no choice but to watch as the sugar comes to a boil. Instead, use a good thermometer to check; when the cooking sugar reaches 285°F (141°C), it is at the hard ball stage—no guessing! Let's get familiar with the different stages of cooking sugar and understand how they affect desserts. I think by better understanding sugar's moods, you may find answers to some of your long-standing frustrations with confection making.

When cooking sugar, you first need to combine it with some water to bring it to a "wet sand" texture. I've always loved this term. I often close my eyes and imagine running my fingers through the wet sands on the beaches of Maui. The water ratio will vary slightly depending on the recipe, but generally having sugar be 10 to 15 percent of the weight is a good starting point (for example, 3 cups [720 ml] water to 100 g [1/2 cup sugar]). The water will help the sugar melt, allowing it to go through its different heat stages. I usually also add a small amount of corn syrup or glucose syrup. These two syrups, called invert sugars, are made up of much longer chains of molecules than sugar, allowing the final product to retain moisture for a longer period of time and preventing premature crystallization.

When you cook sugar mixed with water directly over a flame, it's important that it doesn't crystallize prematurely. This happens when the sugar crystals don't melt evenly and get agitated before reaching their desired temperature. If you've ever tried to cook sugar to make marshmallows or caramel, and halfway through you had a chunky, opaque mess, you know what I'm talking about. The old-school technique is to continually brush the sides of the saucepan with room-temperature water to prevent crystallization. I don't know about you, but I don't have the patience to watch sugar boil! The following three steps will ensure luscious and crystal-free sugar syrup every time:

1. Mix the sugar and the water gently with your hands, taking care not to get it on the sides of the saucepan. After you obtain a wet-sand texture, use your finger and some water to rub down the sides of the saucepan so there is no sugar there prior to cooking.

2. Place the saucepan over medium-high heat and don't move it—at all—until your thermometer reads the desired temperature. Shaking or stirring the saucepan will not make it cook any faster; it will only upset the sugar, forcing it to crystallize prematurely. If you feel the need to agitate something, reach for your martini shaker.

3. When the sugar starts to cook, cover the saucepan with a lid (or if you don't have a lid, use a metal or glass bowl). As the sugar starts to boil and the water starts to evaporate, it will naturally come down the sides of the saucepan, washing down the excess sugar to prevent crystallization. After the sugar has boiled for about a minute, remove the lid and allow the sugar to cook to the desired temperature.

Sweet Note: Crystallization isn't always a bad thing. Sugar's crystallization is what gives us wonderful textures in jellies, jams, candies, and sauces. The key is to manipulate how and when crystallization occurs to obtain a superior product.

lavender honey agar-agar gems

I *love* these little gems. They are so simple to prepare, and they have a subtle but beautiful pop of flavor and texture. An unexpected surprise. The lavender honey complements the floral notes of the orange flower water perfectly. Also, these are made with agar-agar and are a perfect preparation for vegan desserts. Don't knock it till you try it! **YIELD: APPROXIMATELY FOUR HUNDRED FIFTY $\frac{1}{2}$-IN (12-MM) SQUARES**

---

10 g/5 tsp agar-agar powder

25 g/2 tbsp granulated sugar

730 g/3 cups plus 1 tbsp water

175 g/$\frac{1}{2}$ cup plus 2 tsp lavender honey

15 g/1 tbsp orange flower water

Grated zest of 1 orange
(see page 110)

Brush a 9-by-13-in (22-by-33-cm) baking pan lightly with water and set aside. In a small bowl, use clean fingers or a clean, dry whisk to combine the agar-agar powder and sugar thoroughly; set aside.

In a medium stainless-steel or enamel-coated saucepan, combine the water, honey, orange flower water, and orange zest. Over medium heat, bring the mixture to 122°F (50°C), 3 to 5 minutes, stirring occasionally. Test with a thermometer or your finger—it should feel slightly warm to the touch, like tepid bathwater. Slowly whisk in the agar-agar mixture until it is evenly dissolved. Raise the heat to medium-high and let the mixture come to a rolling boil for 30 seconds, whisking constantly. This will activate the gelling power of the agar-agar.

Place the prepared baking pan on an even surface and pour in the warm mixture. Let set at room temperature for 1 to 2 hours, until the mixture is a jellylike consistency. When you shake the tray, it should respond with a firm wiggle.

Cut the gems into squares, diamonds, or the shapes of your choice. Serve immediately, or store in an airtight container for up to 2 weeks in the refrigerator.

Sweet Note: Agar-agar is a neutral, nonflavored seaweed derivative that acts like gelatin. This recipe is entirely vegan and is a wonderful option for vegan sweet freaks. You can find agar-agar at health food stores or online.

burnt caramel sauce

Let's be honest: Few things in the culinary world go together as beautifully as dark caramel and sea salt. The perfect caramel sauce will be sweet and bitter with a hint of salt. This sauce is purely addictive. It's essential to use a good-quality sea salt to impart beautiful mineral flavors to the caramel and further enhance its flavor. Caramel sauce is always good to have on hand for plated desserts, to stir into your morning latte, or as a dip for Granny Smith apple slices. **YIELD: 4 CUPS (960 ML)**

---

1 vanilla bean or 12 g/1 tbsp vanilla bean paste (see Sources, page 216)

500 g/2 cups plus 2 tbsp heavy cream

100 g/¹/₃ cup plus 2 tbsp water

20 g/1 tbsp corn syrup or glucose syrup (see Sources, page 216)

500 g/2¹/₂ cups granulated sugar

12 g/1 tbsp plus 2 tsp fleur de sel

Split the vanilla bean in half lengthwise with a paring knife, and then use the knife to scrape the seeds from the pod. Place the seeds and the pod or the vanilla bean paste in a medium saucepan with the heavy cream over high heat. Bring the cream to a boil, whisking constantly. Boil for 30 seconds and then remove the saucepan from the heat and cover to keep warm.

In a separate, medium stainless-steel or enamel-coated sauce pan, gently combine the water, corn syrup, and sugar with clean fingertips. Place the pan over medium-high heat; when the mixture starts to boil, cover the saucepan with a lid or a bowl and cook for about a minute. (See "Cooking Sugar," page 26.) Remove the lid and continue to cook without stirring, until the mixture reaches 392°F (200°C), turns dark amber, and starts to smoke slightly.

When the mixture reaches 392°F (200°C), turn the heat to low. Remove the vanilla pod from the cream and very carefully pour one-third of the hot cream into the caramelized sugar, slowly whisking with a wire whisk. Be careful not to burn your hand (an oven mitt or heat-resistant glove works great), as the cream will release hot steam. Gradually add the remainder of the hot cream in two stages, then add the fleur de sel, whisking continuously during and after each addition. Once all the cream and salt have been added, bring the heat back to medium and whisk the caramel sauce to ensure that it is evenly mixed. Remove from the heat and strain through a fine-mesh sieve.

The hot caramel sauce can be served immediately. To store, cool to room temperature and keep in an airtight container in the refrigerator for up to 1 month.

butterscotch sauce

Butterscotch is caramel's darker counterpart. It's sultry! I love butterscotch, because when cooked to a high temperature, the molasses in the brown sugar lends a deep, complex flavor to the sauce. Traditional butterscotch sauce uses Scotch whisky, but I use cognac for a sweeter, more elegant note. **YIELD: 4^1/$_2$ CUPS (1 L)**

---

1 vanilla bean or 12 g/1 tbsp vanilla bean paste (see Sources, page 216)

300 g/1^1/$_4$ cups heavy cream

100 g/^{1}/$_3$ cup plus 2 tbsp water

65 g/^{1}/$_4$ cup plus 1 tbsp corn syrup or glucose syrup (see Sources, page 216)

160 g/^{3}/$_4$ cup packed light brown sugar

5 g/heaping 1 tsp granulated sugar

350 g/1^1/$_2$ cups unsalted butter at room temperature

55 g/^{1}/$_4$ cup cognac

5 g/2 tsp Maldon sea salt

Split the vanilla bean in half lengthwise with a paring knife, and then use the knife to scrape the seeds from the pod. Place the seeds and pod or the vanilla bean paste in a medium saucepan with the heavy cream over high heat. Bring the cream to a boil, whisking constantly. Boil for 30 seconds and then remove the saucepan from the heat and cover to keep warm.

In a separate, medium stainless-steel or enamel-coated saucepan, gently combine the water, corn syrup, and both sugars with clean fingertips. Place the pan over medium-low heat and cover with a lid or bowl for about 1 minute to allow the evaporating water to clean the sides of the saucepan. (See "Cooking Sugar," page 26.) Remove the lid and continue cooking without stirring until the mixture reaches 245° to 265°F (120° to 130°C), and begins to smoke—don't worry! This is a sign that the sugars are caramelizing.

Once it starts to smoke, continue cooking and gently stirring with a wooden spoon or a heat-resistant spatula, scraping the bottom of the pot to ensure that the sugars don't prematurely burn. When the mixture reaches 285°F (140°C), turn the heat to low and carefully whisk in the butter, whisking until it's all incorporated. Remove the vanilla pod from the cream, then add the cream to the sugar mixture, stirring gently. Beware: The mixture may spatter and bubble up; keep stirring and soon you'll have thick, rich butterscotch. An oven mitt or heat-proof glove on your stirring hand for this step will prevent burns.

Remove the mixture from the heat and add the cognac and salt, mixing until thoroughly combined. The butterscotch can be served immediately. To store, cool to room temperature and keep in an airtight container in the refrigerator for up to 1 month.

honey molasses candied almonds

The sweet coating and a perfect pinch of sea salt combine with toasted almond flavor to create an addictive treat. I like to have a stash of these to set out for guests on a cheese board. Play around with your favorite nuts in this recipe.

YIELD: 3 CUPS (500 G)

500 g/2 cups plus 2 tbsp water	20 g/1 tbsp honey
500 g/2½ cups granulated sugar	5 g/½ tsp unsulfured molasses
455 g/1 lb blanched whole almonds	1 large pinch Maldon sea salt

Line a 9-by-13-in (23-by-33-cm) baking pan with a Silpat or parchment paper. Set an oven rack to the center position and preheat the oven to 350°F (180°C).

In a medium stainless-steel or enamel-coated saucepan, combine the water and sugar. Place the saucepan over high heat, and when the mixture comes to a rolling boil, immediately turn the heat to medium. When the sugar is fully dissolved, about 30 seconds, turn the heat to medium-low.

Add the almonds to the saucepan and poach for 30 to 45 seconds to blanch them. Strain through a fine-mesh sieve. Pour the almonds into a large mixing bowl and let cool. When they are still warm to the touch but not hot, about 5 minutes, the almonds are ready to work with again.

While the almonds are cooling, combine the honey and molasses in a separate, small bowl. Microwave the mixture for 15 to 30 seconds, until it is viscous and easy to mix. Stir gently to combine. Alternatively, place the honey and molasses in a small saucepan over medium heat and stir constantly for 2 to 3 minutes, or until heated through and easy to stir.

Pour the honey mixture over the almonds and toss gently until the almonds are evenly coated. Sprinkle the sea salt over the nuts and toss to coat. Spread the almonds evenly in the prepared baking pan. Toast in the oven for 10 to 12 minutes. Every 4 to 6 minutes, gently shake the pan so that the almonds roll around and cook evenly. When the almonds are golden brown, remove the pan from the oven and place it on a cooling rack. Cool completely.

Once cool, the almonds are ready to serve, or store in an airtight container in a cool, dry place for 1 to 2 weeks.

Sweet Note: This recipe can be used with most nuts, including hazelnuts or pistachios or even pumpkin seeds. The molasses lends a complex flavor to these sweet little nuggets.

pistachio–vietnamese cinnamon brittle

This may cause cavities, but it is well worth it. A classic candy preparation, this brittle is simple to make and absolutely addictive. Use it as a garnish or break it up into larger pieces, pile it into cellophane bags, and send to friends as treats. The green pistachios spread through the brown brittle give a sweet, nutty flavor and a mosaic look to the crunchy confection, while the Vietnamese cinnamon lends a distinctive warm spicy flavor, making this a more mature candy. I like to fill an airtight container with smaller pieces and keep it within reach for a little bit of tasty brittle as a treat throughout the day. In my kitchen at Tout Sweet you often hear people saying, "I have to walk away from the brittle." **YIELD: 6 TO 8 SERVINGS**

---

350 g/2³/₄ cups whole, shelled green pistachios

4 g/1 tsp Maldon sea salt

8 g/1¹/₂ tbsp ground Vietnamese cinnamon (see Sources, page 216)

2 g/¹/₂ tsp baking soda

5 g/scant 1¹/₂ tsp vanilla bean paste (see Sources, page 216)

350 g/1³/₄ cups granulated sugar

120 g/¹/₂ cup water

75 g/3 tbsp plus 2 tsp corn syrup or glucose syrup (see Sources, page 216)

225 g/1 cup unsalted butter at room temperature

Preheat the oven to 200°F (95°C). Line a baking sheet with parchment paper and spread the pistachios on the sheet. Toast in the oven for about 7 minutes; they should be crispy but still green.

In a small bowl, combine the sea salt, Vietnamese cinnamon, baking soda, and vanilla bean paste. Line a second baking sheet with a Silpat or parchment paper and spray the lining with canola oil. (You may have made brittle in the past with aluminum foil lining. I highly recommend that you give up this tradition, as the foil will stick to your brittle and you may be picking it out for the next 75 hours—or so it might seem.)

In a stainless-steel or enamel-coated 8-qt (7.5-L) saucepan, combine the sugar, water, and corn syrup (see "Cooking Sugar," page 26). Make sure the sides of the saucepan are clean of sugar and cook over high heat, covered, until the mixture starts to boil. Remove the lid and continue to cook until it reaches 250°F (120°C). Turn the

CONTINUED . . .

heat to medium and whisk in the butter until evenly emulsified. Turn the heat to medium-high and keep stirring and cooking until the mixture is a nutty golden brown. Once it has reached the golden-brown pinnacle of brittle perfection, remove from the heat, add the cinnamon mixture, and continue to stir. Take care, as it will bubble up because of the baking soda. Fear not; this is what gives the candy its snappy texture.

Use a rubber spatula to fold in the pistachios until evenly mixed. Immediately pour the mixture directly on top of the lined baking sheet and use an offset spatula to spread it onto the sheet. Put another Silpat or sheet of sprayed parchment paper, sprayed-side down, on top of the brittle and, while still warm, use a rolling pin to roll it out to a nice, even layer. Stop rolling when the brittle is the thickness of the pistachios to create an even mosaic of pistachios.

Remove the top lining and let cool at room temperature, for at least 1 hour. Break into small pieces to enjoy immediately. Use as a garnish or to fill gift bags. Store in an airtight container in a cool, dry place for up to 2 weeks.

hazelnut spears

These decorative garnishes are so fun! I really enjoy making Hazelnut Spears with novice cooks because it shows how much creativity you can have with sugar, even if you're not a trained pastry chef. They are wonderful for garnishing celebration cakes, as well as adding flair to plated desserts. It was after I added these as a garnish that the Sexy Chocolate Coupe (page 210) got its name. **YIELD: 20 SPEARS**

20 whole, raw hazelnuts

500 g/2^1/$_2$ cups granulated sugar

125 g/^{1}/$_2$ cup water

20 g/1 tbsp corn syrup or glucose syrup (see Sources, page 216)

SPECIAL EQUIPMENT:

Two 1-qt (960-ml) mason jars (or other large, sturdy jars)

12-by-12-in (30-by-30-cm) foam core board

20 toothpicks

To set up a place to suspend the spears, line a baking sheet with a Silpat or parchment paper. Set two large mason jars on the baking sheet. Put the foam core board on top of the jars. Set this apparatus in a safe location on a counter or table.

Prepare each hazelnut by using a toothpick to gently skewer it at the indent of the nut. Roll the toothpick between your thumb and forefinger as you insert it just far enough to hold the nut. Fill a medium mixing bowl, large enough to hold bottom of a medium stainless-steel or enamel-coated saucepan, with ice water.

In the saucepan, combine the sugar, water, and corn syrup. (See "Cooking Sugar," page 26.) Place the saucepan over medium-high heat and cook, covered, until the mixture boils and then takes on a light golden-brown color, about 485°F (200°C). Turn off the heat and let the mixture sit, uncovered, for 30 seconds. It will continue cooking and become a dark amber color. Submerge the bottom of the saucepan in the ice water for 10 seconds to stop the cooking. Remove the pan from the ice water and gently swirl the saucepan around. The mixture should resemble maple sap—dark and thick. Set the pan on an even surface.

Work quickly, with one hazelnut at a time. Dip a hazelnut into the mixture until just covered, pull it straight up out of the sugar mixture, and move it over to the foam core board. The sugar will continue to drip. Pierce the toothpick into the underside of the foam core board so that the sugar drips away from the board and onto the prepared baking sheet. Repeat with all the hazelnuts and allow them to dry and harden for at least 15 minutes. Use sharp, clean scissors to snip the sugar spears to the desired length.

CONTINUED . . .

When ready to use, gently remove each hazelnut from the toothpick with a wiggling motion. These dramatic hazelnuts are best if used immediately, but they can be prepared up to 2 days in advance and stored still on the toothpicks, with parchment paper to separate them, in an airtight container in a cool, dry place.

Sweet Note: Hot sugar dripping in your kitchen can get very messy. Have everything set up before you start. Set up a station for yourself at the kitchen table or counter where you can dip the hazelnuts and then poke the toothpicks into the foam core without having to move very far. Placing some newspaper below the area where you will be dipping the nuts into the sugar will make cleaning a lot easier.

BUTTER & FLOUR

Buddhists believe that we can experience momentary glimpses of enlightenment, a brief period during which all seems to fit in its place and we feel a sense of calm and understanding—

a moment when all seems right in the world.

This is precisely the unspoken harmony that exists between butter and flour. Simple in their color and flavor, they remind us, in working together, of the beauty of empty space, of the negative in the positive, of coming together and letting go. We dream of crêpes with their light, airy texture or of a good génoise cake that is riddled with air pockets and bounces back to the touch. These two ingredients are ubiquitous in Western kitchens, and once you know their special qualities, you can play with them and bring their beauty to entirely new levels. For starters, if you've never "cut" cold butter into flour with your bare hands, feeling the tender give of the pliable butter into the powdery piles of flour, I highly suggest you give it a go.

When butter and flour come together, a little bit of heaven comes to earth. Cold butter incorporated into flour steams and pushes up the gluten strands, creating air pockets. Room-temperature butter is often just right for creaming with sugar to make cookie dough and tarts. The creaming pulls some of the water out of the butter, making room for the flour, so that the dough is creamy and rich before going into the oven. Butter melted and mixed well with flour creates a souplike batter for crêpes that spreads and stays light and airy in the pan. The butter in crêpes also brings fat and protein to the party, crisping up on the heat and creating the golden-brown hue that every baker aims for.

The first rule of thumb when you're buying for baking is to choose unsalted butter. If you're going to serve the butter fresh or are working with a small, delicate recipe, choose a creamy, freshly churned type such as European-style butter. I always choose organic so that I know there are no added chemicals, from the way the cow has been raised and fed to the treatment of the milk and butter. Whenever possible, my butter comes from a local, organic dairy farmer. What the cows eat matters in the final taste and quality of the product.

the state of the butter

Baking with butter is a state of mind, and of temperature. I cannot stress this enough. At Tout Sweet, all my cooks know how meticulous I am about the different temperatures for different applications of butter. Has it been held at room temperature, kept cold, frozen, or melted ahead of time? Butter is not thermo-reversible. In other words, once butter has been melted, it won't go back to its original state. Butter melts above 82°F (32°C), so on a hot summer day "room temperature" can lead to "melted butter mess."

COLD BUTTER—37° to 41°F (3° to 5°C). Layered and flaky dough begins with cold butter. The most elegant example of a layered dough is the croissant, a buttery, layered, crunchy-on-the-outside, soft-on-the-inside masterpiece of the butter and flour marriage. A croissant requires butter that has been treated right throughout its life so that it retains its integrity, with the milk solids fully suspended in the water and fat. A recipe for layered dough will usually call for cold, cubed butter. This is the best form for butter that will be cut into flour, or mixed with flour until the butter is in pearl-size pieces. When butter is cut into a dough and kept cold and chunky in the midst of the dough, it steams as it bakes in the hot oven and creates an incredible layered, flaky pastry. This technique is used for biscuits, scones, and flaky pie crusts. When done right, the steam from the cold butter will push against the soft sides of the dough as the product bakes, and the rest of the butter will melt into the biscuit or croissant. Anytime you are going for flaky, layered pastries, remember: Put cold butter into a hot oven. If the dough begins to warm before it's ready for baking, put it into the freezer for about 10 minutes to bring the temperature back down. Your results will be amazing and magical.

ROOM-TEMPERATURE BUTTER—66° to 69°F (19° to 21°C). Butter's interaction with flour and leavening agents is the key to the structure of your baked goods. Butter that is emulsified with sugar, or creamed, is the perfect beginning to most classic cookie recipes. If a recipe calls for blending room-temperature butter in your stand mixer as an early step, give the mixer time to whip the butter into submission. A creamed, well-blended butter will turn a lighter shade of yellow as it fills with air pockets. These air pockets are the future home of the rest of the ingredients and make the structure of the crispy-edged, gooey-centered cookie that reminds many of us of being home for the holidays. To achieve a creamed butter, always have it at room temperature before you begin. You will find I talk a lot about emulsifying butter into various ganaches, curds, and custards, and when I do this I always use room-temperature butter.

MELTED BUTTER—82° to 95°F (32° to 35°C). Butter is melted for recipes that use the butter for its protein and flavor; a crêpe recipe is a great example of this. The crêpe's defining element is its flatness, so the leavening aspect of butter would work against the crêpe's beauty.

In addition to adding flavor, fat, and protein to the crêpe batter, melted butter helps the crêpe to brown in the pan.

The addition of heat changes most food ingredients, and butter is a clear example of this. Once heated, the butter looks different, is in a completely different state (liquid instead of solid), and won't go back to the way it was. Melted butter is the beginning of clarified butter (also called drawn butter), the golden, translucent oil that sits on top of the sunny yellow, opaque butter solids.

The other not-so-secret wonder of melting butter is to continue to cook it until it reaches a beautiful brown color. Brown butter, also called *beurre noisette*, is a nutty, flavorful addition to some classic pastry recipes and is used in savory dishes as a sauce base. To make brown butter, melt butter over medium heat and then keep cooking until it boils and bubbles and the butter solids begin to brown. There's a fine line between brown nuttiness and burnt bitterness, so keep your eye on it.

flour

It took Europeans many generations to fully grind and refine wheat into the powdery white flour that we know and love today. Once they learned how to make the *fleur de farine*, however, cakes and tarts were not far away. I am constantly amazed by the many uses of flour, from the stretchy, developed gluten recipes that give us breads to the flaky, tender treatments that result in tarts and biscuits. Much has been said and written about the healthfulness, or lack thereof, of white flour. I, for one,

would not want to live in a world where I couldn't bite into flaky, tender, sweet shortcake. All things in moderation.

Most professional bakers pay attention to the level of gluten in the flour they are working with. The level of gluten has to do with the wheat the flour is derived from. Different types of baked goods call for flours with different gluten levels, which the mills produce by using hard or soft wheats or by blending them in different proportions.

ALL-PURPOSE FLOUR. All-purpose flour is exactly what Goldilocks would be looking for if she stumbled into a bakery instead of the bears' house—it's just right. It's a combination of hard and soft wheat, meaning that the proteins in all-purpose flour develop into both short and long strands when mixed with liquid and fat and kneaded. This is the flour to have on hand at home. Different flour producers use different ratios of hard and soft wheat. In fact, the same producer might shift the ratio seasonally to keep prices down. If you're going to use all-purpose flour for yeast bread, check the label and choose one with 2 to 4 grams of protein per ¼ cup of flour.

HIGH-GLUTEN FLOUR. Sometimes labeled as bread flour, this is the high-gluten and high-protein product that leads to the joyful, elastic bliss of kneading well-formed bread dough. The high gluten content comes from hard wheat, and the flour will feel more granular when rubbed between your fingers. Any time you are working with yeast or other baked goods that will stretch and pull before and after they come out of the oven, work with high-gluten flour.

LOW-GLUTEN FLOUR. This flour, also called cake flour, is low in gluten, low in protein, and comes from soft wheat. Tarts, croissants, and cakes benefit from the shorter strands that low-gluten flour produces. Working with low-gluten flour in your batters and tart dough will counter-act a little bit of overmixing. The name *shortbread* comes from the shortness or crispness of this dough. Whereas high-gluten dough snaps back like an elastic band when pulled, low-gluten dough breaks relatively quickly when pulled.

GLUTEN-FREE FLOUR MIXES. We are living in a time when people are interested in how food affects their bodies and what can be done about the negative health effects of certain foods. The most positive thing about this trend, from this pastry chef's perspective, is that we increasingly have access to flours from nuts, starches, and grains other than wheat. If you or a loved one is on a low-gluten or gluten-free diet, there are some amazing recipes available. I've had a lot of success with recipes from cultures that don't use wheat as a staple. Japanese recipes rely on rice as the favored starch, so Japanese desserts are often naturally gluten-free. The best way to learn about these different flours is to play with them. My favorite gluten-free flour mix comes from King Arthur Flour (see Sources, page 216). But there are many different mixes available—try some out or make your own.

・ ・ ・

The beautiful balance of butter and flour brings us air and solid matter in one recipe. Although they can each stand on their own, together they hold each other up to new heights. The physical interaction of these two partners brings us some of life's sweetest delights. With butter and flour we get the thin delicacy of a crêpe, an open vessel for myriad fillings; and we also get buttery, flaky shortcake, a perfect pairing for fruits and creams. When used correctly and appreciated in their different states of being, flour and butter elevate desserts with their singular simplicity.

salty hazelnut & brown sugar crumble

These nutty, crumbly, salty, sweet, and buttery little nuggets are on my list of top-ten pastry must-have-on-hand items. As simple as this recipe is, the ingredients together create really scrumptious morsels. The hazelnuts add an additional crunch, and the flake sea salt awakens your palate. I keep some of this in my freezer at all times, ready to bake off. It's great for topping your breakfast muffins before baking, or as the top layer of parfaits and petits fours for flavor and crunch. If you really want to make this crumble addictive, once it is baked and cooled to room temperature, toss it with a little bit of melted gianduja. **YIELD: 6 CUPS (1 KG)**

---

220 g/1 cup unsalted butter

220 g/1 cup plus 2 tbsp packed light brown sugar

5 g/2 tsp Maldon sea salt

220 g/1^1/$_2$ cups plus 1 tbsp all-purpose flour

220 g/2^1/$_2$ cups plus 1 tbsp almond flour

110 g/1 cup finely chopped hazelnuts

Bring all ingredients to room temperature by setting them out on the counter about 1 hour before baking. Preheat the oven to 325°F (165°C).

In a stand mixer fitted with the paddle attachment, cream the butter, brown sugar, and salt on medium speed until just evenly mixed. Turn off the mixer. Add both flours to the mixer bowl and, on low speed, mix everything together until it combines into a soft paste, about 30 seconds. Add the hazelnuts and mix until evenly combined, about 30 seconds more.

Use a cross-wire cooling rack to cut the dough into crumbles. Place the rack over a baking sheet lined with parchment paper. Press the dough into a rectangle 1/4 in (6 mm) thick, and place it on the rack. With clean hands, force the dough through the holes of the rack. Alternatively, you can press the dough into a 1/4-in- (6-mm-) thick disk on a cutting board, then use a metal bench scraper or sharp knife to chop the dough into small pieces. (The uncooked crumbles can be stored in an airtight container in the freezer for up to 1 month.)

To bake, scatter the crumbles evenly on a rimmed baking sheet lined with parchment paper, and bake for 5 to 7 minutes, tossing once halfway through, until the crumbles begin to turn from golden to light brown. Cool to room temperature and store in an airtight container for up to 5 days.

paper-thin crêpes

Crêpes always remind me of Paris, so naturally I have a distinct fondness for them. Whenever I make them at home for friends and loved ones, whether for breakfast or for dessert, there is always a romantic nostalgia to the process. They are made with love! This recipe uses equal weights flour and cornstarch, which makes for a very delicate, paper-thin, delicious, and tender batter. When I'm making them, I tend to eat a few crêpes during the cooking process, sprinkled with sugar and a bit of fresh orange zest on top. When warm, these little guys are what simple, sweet pleasures are all about! **YIELD: ABOUT 30 CRÊPES**

300 g/6 whole eggs

800 g/3¹/₃ cups whole milk

25 g/2 tbsp granulated sugar

2 g/heaping ¹/₄ tsp kosher salt

100 g/³/₄ cup all-purpose flour

100 g/³/₄ cup plus 1 tbsp cornstarch

100 g/¹/₂ cup unsalted butter

Set the eggs and milk on the counter 1 hour before baking to come to room temperature. In a large mixing bowl, combine the sugar, salt, flour, and cornstarch and use a whisk to mix together. Melt the butter in a small saucepan over low heat.

In a medium bowl, combine the milk and eggs, using a whisk or handheld blender to break up the eggs and incorporate them into the milk. It should become a thick, pale yellow, glossy liquid. Slowly add the melted butter and mix to combine.

Make a well in the center of the dry mixture, and then, while whisking, slowly pour the wet ingredients into the well. A good option is to use a handheld blender to ensure even mixing. The batter will be the consistency of a soupy stew—wet but thick. Allow the batter to rest at room temperature for 1 hour; this will lead to crêpes that are tender, not chewy.

Heat an 8-in (20-cm) nonstick pan over medium heat until hot to the touch. Coat with cooking spray or pour in a small amount of canola oil and swirl to coat. With one hand, hold on to the handle of the pan. With the other hand, ladle ¹/₄ cup (60 ml) of the crêpe batter into the pan. Constantly move the pan in a circular motion so that the pan is evenly coated with the batter. This will create a thin, even crêpe.

When the pan is evenly coated with batter, return it to the burner over medium-low heat. Cook until the top has just set and begins to form bubbles, 1 to 2 minutes. To check doneness, peek under the crêpe by gently lifting it with your spatula. When the bottom is golden brown, with darker spots all over, use your fingers to flip the crêpe over quickly and cook for an additional 30 seconds. Remove from the pan and place on a plate.

CONTINUED . . .

Continue this method for each crêpe. Place parchment paper between the crêpes so they do not stick together.

The crêpes are ready to be served immediately or used to create a multilayered crêpe cake (see page 204) and served as dessert. Crêpes can be made in advance and set aside in the refrigerator for up to 2 days. Be sure to separate them with parchment paper and cover completely with plastic wrap.

Sweet Note: After the first side is cooked, use your fingers to flip the crêpe over. I promise this will end up being much easier than using a spatula or tongs. Don't be afraid of the flip—just move quickly. The warm crêpes can be served with some simple sliced peaches or nectarines and topped with a dollop of Vanilla Bean Chantilly (page 81).

moist chocolate chunk cookies with flake sea salt

These are a wonderful sweet treat, with a couple of small shifts to the classic chocolate chip cookie recipe. A sure way to put a smile on friends' faces, be they nine or ninety. There are days that I try to be inconspicuous at Tout Sweet (a "secret shopper" of sorts), and it is a joy to watch people's faces light up as they bite into this simple cookie. Chocolate chip cookies aren't a part of the culture in Turkey, and my *anne* (mom), an amazing baker, never made them when I was growing up. But I imagine that Americans' dessert nostalgia must involve a buttery, gooey, chocolaty cookie like this one. **YIELD: 40 COOKIES**

---

210 g/1½ cups all-purpose flour

5 g/½ tsp baking soda

3 g/½ tsp kosher salt

345 g/12 oz 64% to 70% dark chocolate

½ vanilla bean or 6 g/1½ tsp vanilla bean paste (see Sources, page 216)

145 g/⅔ cup unsalted butter at room temperature

115 g/½ cup plus heaping 1 tbsp granulated sugar

115 g/½ cup packed light brown sugar

100 g/2 whole eggs

5 g/2 tsp Maldon sea salt

Preheat the oven to 325°F (165°C). Line a baking sheet with parchment paper. Sift the flour, baking soda, and kosher salt over a large bowl or piece of parchment paper; set aside. Break the chocolate into ¼- to ½-in (6- to 12-mm) pieces, divide into two equal piles, and set aside. Split the vanilla bean in half lengthwise with a paring knife and then use the knife to scrape the seeds from the pod. Discard the pod or reserve for use in another recipe for added vanilla flavor.

In a stand mixer fitted with the paddle attachment, at high speed, combine the butter, the seeds scraped from the vanilla bean or the vanilla bean paste, and both sugars; beat until fully combined and the color begins to change to a lighter shade of yellow. (Do not overwhip.) As soon as the color starts to change, slow the speed of the mixer and add the eggs; beat until fully incorporated. Add the flour mixture and CONTINUED . . .

mix until just incorporated. Add one pile of the chocolate and mix until just combined.

Use a #24 scoop to scoop 2-in (5-cm) balls of the dough onto the parchment paper–lined baking sheet. Sprinkle each cookie with a small amount of the sea salt, and stand a piece of chocolate up in the top of each ball. Bake for 5 minutes, turn the pan 180 degrees, and bake for another 5 minutes, until the center is gooey and the edges are crispy. As soon as you take the baking sheet out of the oven, slam it against the counter to remove any air bubbles and encourage gooey, not doughy, cookies. Use a metal spatula to set the warm cookies on a cooling rack, and let cool for 5 to 10 minutes.

Sweet Note: I like my cookies flat and gooey instead of doughy and filled with air. The trick to getting them this way is to not whip too much air into the batter and to smack the baking sheet against your counter just after removing it from the oven.

crème fraîche shortcakes

Shortcakes, scones, biscuits—they all come from the same heritage. When I was a young cook baking these shortcakes, people would refer to them as scones, and I'd get furious. But now I just think: Delicious is delicious! These shortcakes are a real delight. I use crème fraîche instead of heavy cream or milk, which creates moist yet crumbly and delicate shortcakes with an enjoyable tang. The trick here is to not overmix. I encourage you to mix the dough by hand with a wooden spoon and bowl. If you love your mixer and want to use it anyway, stop after you've added all the ingredients and the dough is 75 percent combined, then pour it onto your table and shape the shortcakes by hand. Trust me; the love you put into them will come through in the end.

These babies literally break apart and crumble, and they are perfect for dipping or smothering in summer fruit sauces. I like to use them in my strawberry shortcake (see page 200), to soak up the delicious strawberry–pinot noir sauce, or you can serve them immediately with farm butter and homemade preserves. **YIELD: ABOUT 12 SHORTCAKES**

---

95 g/$^1\!/_2$ cup cold unsalted butter

405 g/$2^3\!/_4$ cups plus 1 tbsp all-purpose flour

100 g/$^1\!/_2$ cup granulated sugar, plus 50 g/$^1\!/_4$ cup

25 g/$1^3\!/_4$ tbsp baking powder

2 g/heaping $^1\!/_4$ tsp kosher salt

6 g/$1^1\!/_2$ tsp ground green cardamom

370 g/$1^1\!/_2$ cups crème fraîche

2 g/$^1\!/_2$ tsp vanilla bean paste (see Sources, page 216)

Grated zest of 1 orange (see page 110)

About 120 g/$^1\!/_2$ cup heavy cream

Cut the butter into $^1\!/_2$-in (12-mm) cubes; reserve in the refrigerator. Sift the flour, the 100 g/$^1\!/_2$ cup sugar, baking powder, salt, and cardamom together over a piece of parchment paper. In a medium bowl, combine the crème fraîche, vanilla bean paste, and orange zest; reserve in the refrigerator.

CONTINUED . . .

In a large mixing bowl, combine the sifted dry ingredients and cold, cubed butter. Use your fingertips to gently coat the butter with flour. Use a wooden spoon to mix until it looks like Parmesan cheese.

Add the reserved crème fraîche mixture. Continue to stir until the batter is 75 percent combined. Some dry flour and butter will line the outside of the bowl. Lightly flour a flat, clean workspace and pour the contents of the bowl onto the floured workspace. Knead gently with the heel of your hand to combine the ingredients. When the dough begins to form, becomes more silky, and holds itself together, cut the dough ball in half with a bench scraper or large knife, and then gently sprinkle any stray dry ingredients on top of one half of the dough. Place the second half of the dough on top of the first half to incorporate the dry ingredients, and push down. Layering the dough ball in this way keeps the layers flaky; do this two to three times. Shortcakes are best when they're flaky and buttery. The secret is to not overwork the dough—be willing to walk away. When all the dry ingredients are incorporated, stop layering. Press the dough into a 2-in- (5-cm-) thick block, wrap it with plastic wrap, and chill it in the refrigerator for at least 2 hours.

Preheat the oven to 325°F (165°C). Line a baking sheet with parchment paper.

Pull the dough from the refrigerator and unwrap it onto a lightly floured work surface; lightly flour the top of the dough. Shape the dough into a rectangle and use a rolling pin to beat the dough several times, making indents along the top. This will begin to soften the dough without overworking it. Sandwich the rectangle of dough between two pieces of parchment paper to make the process of rolling out easier. Roll the dough from the center out into a $^1/_2$-in- (12-mm-) thick rectangle. As much as possible, work from the center out in one direction with your rolling pin; shortcakes stay flakier the less you work the dough. To make sure that the dough is rolled out evenly, run clean hands under the dough and feel for thick spots. It is likely that the center will be the thickest; if so, take one swipe of the rolling pin across the center. Use a bench scraper or cookie cutter to cut the dough into equilateral triangles or shapes of your choice. Once they are cut, the shortcakes are ready to be baked. (They can also be put into an airtight container or wrapped tightly in plastic wrap and stored in the freezer for up to 2 weeks—it is always nice to have something in your freezer to bake when a spontaneous gathering happens or you're invited to dinner at a friend's house.)

Lay the shortcake triangles onto the prepared baking sheet, lightly brush the tops with heavy cream, then generously sprinkle the remaining 50 g/$^1/_4$ cup granulated sugar onto the top in a mound so that they will have a wonderful sweet and crunchy crust. Bake in the preheated oven for 10 minutes, turn the baking sheet 180 degrees, and bake for another 8 to 10 minutes, until golden brown on both top and bottom. They should lift easily off the parchment paper. If the oven you are working with is aggressive, place the baking sheet onto a second baking sheet to prevent the bottoms from burning.

The shortcakes are ready to be served immediately. Alternatively, you can store them in an airtight container in a cool, dry place for up to 3 days. If you store them, I recommend refreshing them in a 325°F (165°C) oven for 5 minutes to recrisp them before serving.

Sweet Note: Triangles are my favorite shape because I'm into clean edges, but feel free to be creative with the shapes of your shortcakes. Use a cookie cutter or your bench scraper to cut the dough into interesting shapes. When making your choice, think about the plate you'll be serving the shortcakes on and how to present the final product in a beautiful way.

sweet almond tart shells

A flaky, buttery tart crust acts as the edible plate for juicy, ripe fruit or a silky, luscious pastry cream. This tart dough is truly fantastic. It has almond flour to add another layer of yum. When baked to GBD (golden brown and delicious) and fresh out of the oven, it fills the kitchen with an aroma that is sure to entice everyone's sweet tooth.

YIELD: THREE 10-IN (25-CM) TART SHELLS OR EIGHTEEN 3-IN (8-CM) TART SHELLS

---

1 vanilla bean or 12 g/1 tbsp vanilla bean paste (see Sources, page 216)

300 g/1¼ cups unsalted butter at room temperature

5 g/¾ tsp kosher salt

175 g/1½ cups powdered sugar

60 g/⅓ cup granulated sugar

60 g/¾ cup almond flour

550 g/4 cups all-purpose flour

Filling of your choice

Split the vanilla bean in half lengthwise with a paring knife and then use the knife to scrape the seeds from the pod. Discard the pod or reserve for use in another recipe.

In a large mixing bowl, combine the butter, salt, both sugars, almond flour, seeds scraped from the vanilla bean or the vanilla bean paste, and 175 g/1⅓ cups of the all-purpose flour. Use a wooden spoon to blend into a thin, creamlike batter; don't overmix. Fold in the remaining 375 g/2⅔ cups all-purpose flour until just combined. You should have something that looks and feels like cream-colored play-dough. Do not overwork. Turn the dough out of the bowl and onto a counter; use your hands to form a thick disk, about 6 in (15 cm) in diameter and 2 in (5 cm) thick. Cut into three even pieces, and then re-form into 2-in- (5-cm-) thick disks. Wrap the dough disks well in plastic wrap.

Refrigerate for at least 2 hours, but no more than 24 hours.

When the dough is ready to work, preheat the oven to 300°F (150°C). Coat tart pans with cooking spray or butter. Put a small amount of flour into the oiled tart pans and shake to coat; discard the excess flour.

Working with one dough disk at a time, flour both sides of the disk and sandwich between two pieces of thick parchment paper. Gently beat the top of the dough with your rolling pin to soften. When the dough is softened, work from the center of the disk out so that you do not develop the gluten too much; this will result in flaky, tender tart shells. Roll the rolling pin over the top of the top piece of parchment paper to keep the dough from sticking and make it easier to roll out evenly. Roll until the

CONTINUED . . .

dough is paper-thin. Don't cut corners here; take your time, and roll it out very thin—$\frac{1}{8}$ in (4 mm). To check for even thickness, gently lift the dough and run your hands under it. There will likely be a bit of a bulge in the center. Flatten this at the very end by rolling over it.

Cut the dough into a round a bit bigger than the tart pan. Place the dough in the prepared tart pan and use your thumb and forefinger to gently push the dough into the bottom and up the side of the pan, moving in a circular motion around the pan. The dough should stand up just over the edge of the pan once you have set it in. Using a sharp paring knife, with the tart pan as a guide, make a clean cut of the dough so that it is even with the top of the pan. Remove the excess tart dough and use it in another tart shell, or twist it, sprinkle with cinnamon and sugar, and bake for a lovely chef's snack. Place the tart shell in the freezer for at least 15 minutes. This will help keep the dough from falling during baking. Repeat for the remaining dough.

Place the tart shells on a baking sheet and bake for $7\frac{1}{2}$ minutes, then turn them 180 degrees and bake for another 6 to 8 minutes, or until they are golden brown and look flaky. If the bottoms of the shells have bubbled up during baking, immediately push the bubbles down with the back of a spoon during the first rotation.

Remove the tart shells from their pans and place on cooling racks for at least 30 minutes. Once the shells are cool to the touch, they are ready to be filled with in-season fruit or a creamy filling. For a special occasion, try the Cheeky Raspberry Tart on page 196. The baked unfilled tart shells can be stored in an airtight container in the refrigerator for up to 1 week.

citrus-scented almond génoise cake

The génoise, an Italian sponge cake named after the city of Genoa, is a standard in any baker's portfolio. This cake doesn't use chemical leavening, instead relying on air "suspended" in the cake batter before baking. In France, génoise is very common, and the cake *pain de gênes* is essentially the same thing, using copious amounts of almond flour. You could say my recipe is a hybrid of the two. It's a very simple but delicious cake. The addition of orange zest awakens the latent flavors of almonds and eggs while giving the cake a sweet, fruity essence. I love to cut génoise into cubes or strips, toss them lightly in butter and sugar, and then toast them in a 350°F (180°C) oven to make sweet croutons. I use these to add a golden, crunchy, chewy topper to desserts.

YIELD: ONE 9-BY-13-IN (23-BY-33-CM) CAKE

150 g/3 whole eggs	250 g/1¼ cups granulated sugar
60 g/3 egg yolks	Grated zest of 1 orange (see page 110)
270 g/9 egg whites	Grated zest of 1 lemon (see page 110) plus 5 g/1 tsp lemon juice
150 g/⅔ cup almond flour	
120 g/¾ cup plus 2 tbsp all-purpose flour	10 g/2 tsp vanilla bean paste (see Sources, page 216)

Put the eggs on the counter 1 hour before you plan to bake, so that they come to room temperature. Preheat the oven to 350°F (180°C). Line the bottom of a 9-by-13-by-2-in (23-by-33-by-5-cm) baking pan with parchment paper.

Into a large bowl or over a piece of parchment paper, sift together the almond flour and all-purpose flour. Set aside in a large mixing bowl.

Use a stand mixer with the whisk attachment to combine 150 g/¾ cup of the sugar, the whole eggs, egg yolks, orange zest, lemon zest, and vanilla bean paste. Whisk on high speed to

the pale ribbon stage, at which point the batter will have tripled in size and have pale yellow peaks. You don't need to be on high alert; you can't overwhip the mixture. Once mixed, use a rubber spatula to gently transfer the mixture to a large, 4-qt (3.8-L) mixing bowl.

Wash, rinse, and dry the whisk attachment and mixer bowl. Place the egg whites into the mixing bowl and add the lemon juice. Whisk the egg whites and lemon juice on medium speed, stopping just as the mixture is doubled in size. Add the remaining 100 g/½ cup sugar and continue to whip for about 20 seconds more, or until a scoop of the meringue forms a peak and then immediately curls over. This is the soft-peak stage. At this point pay attention; you don't want to overwhip the egg whites (see page 74).

Use a rubber spatula to fold the egg yolk mixture into the sifted dry ingredients until just evenly combined. Gently fold one-third of the egg white meringue into the mixture, then fold in half of what you have left, and then fold in the rest. Take care to not overwork it, so the batter does not deflate. Gently pour the batter into the prepared baking pan. Spread evenly, using an offset spatula.

Bake for approximately 12 minutes, or until the top becomes a light golden brown. Rotate the pan 180 degrees. Bake for another 3 to 5 minutes, until the cake is a deeper golden brown and bounces back to the touch.

Remove the cake from the oven and place on a cooling rack; let cool to room temperature. If you will not be using it immediately, wrap your génoise completely with plastic wrap. The cake can be kept wrapped at room temperature for up to 4 days.

Sweet Note: A génoise is almost as delicate as the infamous soufflé. Keep the oven door closed until a crust forms on top, about 7 minutes. Génoise is known for being a light and fluffy cake, so bake this beauty until just done. Once the cake is out of the oven, it will continue to bake to perfection in the hot pan.

honey baked crispy phyllo squares

I lovingly refer to these as deconstructed baklava blocks. Phyllo is the backbone of many Turkish desserts, and I have fond memories of it. When I was four years old, I would watch in wonder as my mom, my aunts, and my grandma stretched fresh phyllo on the table top and then layered them to make crispy, sweet baklava. Pistachio was always my favorite! Like raising a child, stretching fresh phyllo into its paper-thin wonder really does take a village (or at least a large family). I thank Buddha for good-quality store-bought phyllo every time I pull it out of the freezer.

Phyllo is so wonderfully crisp, and when baked with butter and glazed with the honey syrup, it's addictive! I find this preparation much easier than the traditional baklava, as the squares are more manageable, and they can get really golden brown and crispy. You can use them to give texture to your parfaits, layer as a mille-feuille or napoleon, or even place a lovely stack on a cheese platter. Whatever you do, enjoy them, and imagine that a wide-eyed, four-year-old Yigit is watching you make them. **YIELD: 10 SQUARES**

Grated zest of $^1/_2$ orange (see page 110)

100 g/$^1/_2$ cup granulated sugar, plus more for sprinkling

2 g/2$^1/_2$ tsp ground Ceylon cinnamon

1 g/$^1/_4$ tsp ground green cardamom

6 sheets phyllo dough

100 g/$^2/_3$ cup unsalted butter, melted

40 g/$^1/_4$ cup light honey

Preheat the oven to 325°F (165°C). Line the bottom of a rimmed baking sheet with parchment paper. Clean a 24-by-18-in (60-by-45-cm) cutting board or set up a separate, parchment paper–lined baking sheet. Combine the orange zest with the 100 g/$^1/_2$ cup sugar in a small bowl; with clean hands, rub the orange zest into the sugar to release the essential oils. Add the cinnamon and cardamom to the sugar and mix to combine.

Lay 2 sheets of phyllo dough onto the work surface, use a pastry brush to apply a thin layer of the melted butter, and then sprinkle liberally with a layer of the scented sugar. Lay another 2 sheets of phyllo dough on top of the first layer and press lightly. Add more melted butter and then scented sugar, the final 2 sheets of phyllo, and a final layer of butter and scented sugar. You should have used all the butter and scented sugar by now.

CONTINUED . . .

Cover the layered phyllo completely with damp paper towels, to prevent the fragile dough from drying out and cracking, and place it in the refrigerator for 10 minutes, or until the butter returns to a solid state.

When the butter is cooled to solid, remove the phyllo layers from the refrigerator and remove the paper towels. Use a pizza cutter or a very sharp knife to cut the layers into 2-in (5-cm) squares. Place the squares onto the prepared baking sheet and cover them with another piece of parchment paper. Weigh the top parchment paper down with another baking sheet. Alternatively, you can lay the phyllo squares on a silicone baking sheet and lay another sheet of silicone directly on top to weigh them down.This will ensure that the phyllo squares will puff just enough to be flaky and crispy while still maintaining a crisp, linear look.

Bake for 10 minutes. The squares should begin to lightly brown, especially along the edges. Remove the top baking sheet and rotate the bottom baking sheet 180 degrees, then bake for another 10 to 12 minutes, until the squares caramelize evenly through the center and become crispy, flaky, and golden. Remove from the oven; let cool at room temperature.

While the squares are baking, heat the honey in the microwave for 20 seconds or until liquid and easy to spread. Alternatively, place it in a small saucepan and heat over low heat for 1 minute. When the squares are finished in the oven, brush them very lightly with the warm honey and sprinkle with granulated sugar immediately.

The squares are best served fresh. If needed, you can store them in an airtight container for up to 3 days in a cool, dry place, but if you do this, I recommend waiting to glaze them with the honey until just before serving so that they don't get soggy. Refresh them in the oven before brushing them with the honey.

Sweet Note: When working with phyllo dough, always keep a clean, moist kitchen towel over the sheets when you are not handling them. Phyllo dough is very thin and will dry out quickly, becoming brittle and impossible to work with.

orange-scented waffles with "toffee"

Waffles for dessert, you ask. I say why not!

The inspiration for these waffles comes from Daniel, Daniel Boulud's restaurant in New York City. I was the pastry sous chef at the time, and when we started to play around with this idea, I thought it was bizarre but figured I would at least have a tasty snack along the way. I found that they make a perfect ending to a meal, especially in the summer, with all the wonderful stone fruit available that time of year. The inspiration for the "toffee" came years later when I was recollecting how our master breadmaker at Daniel, Mark Fiorentino, used to make the most delicious panettone studded with crushed brown-sugar cubes. His rendition of this Italian classic was purely addictive, but then again anything Mark touches turns to gold. So I married the two hungry memories, and the result is divine.

Whether you make these for breakfast, which I encourage, or to serve as a dessert to your guests, once the handle on the waffle iron goes down and the sweet aromas fill the air, I'm sure you'll fall in love with them as well. **YIELD: 5 LARGE OR 10 SMALL WAFFLES**

---

335 g/2⅓ cups all-purpose flour

50 g/¼ cup granulated sugar

10 g/1 tsp baking powder

5 g/1 tsp baking soda

2 g/heaping ¼ tsp kosher salt

70 g/⅓ cup grapeseed oil

50 g/1 whole egg, plus 30 g/ 1 egg white

430 g/1¾ cups plus 2 tbsp whole milk

Grated zest of 1 orange (see page 110)

Grated zest of 1 lemon (see page 110)

8 to 10 rough-cut cane sugar cubes

Plug in your waffle iron and preheat it, following the manufacturer's instructions. Sift the flour, granulated sugar, baking powder, baking soda, and salt together into a large bowl. In a separate medium bowl, combine the grapeseed oil, whole egg, milk, orange zest, and lemon zest evenly with a whisk. Pulverize the sugar cubes in a food processor to the consistency of heavy sand and set aside.

CONTINUED . . .

Make a well in the center of the dry ingredients; while whisking, slowly pour the wet ingredients into the dry ingredients. Whisk the batter together until it is silky and evenly combined. Be sure that there are no lumps.

In a separate medium bowl, whisk the egg white to medium stiff peaks. Use a rubber spatula or wooden spoon to gently fold the egg white into the batter just before cooking the waffles. When the waffle iron is hot, coat both sides with cooking spray and then ladle $\frac{1}{3}$ to $\frac{3}{4}$ cup (75 to 180 ml) of batter—depending on the size of your waffle iron—into the center of the iron. The batter should spread from the center out to the sides to an even $\frac{1}{2}$-in- (12-mm-)

thick layer. Sprinkle about 1 tbsp of the ground sugar cubes across the batter. The sugar will caramelize and become toffee-like during cooking. Pull down the top of the iron and cook the waffles, following the manufacturer's directions. If you don't have a modern-day, Jetsons-type waffle iron with all the bells and whistles to tell you when the waffles are cooked, keep them baking until the iron stops steaming and the cooked waffle separates easily from the top of the iron. Immediately remove the waffle from the iron. Stack the waffles on a serving platter and keep them warm while you cook the rest of the waffles.

Serve immediately while warm and fluffy.

EGGS & DAIRY

If butter and flour are the building blocks of many of our favorite baked goods and desserts, the combined world of eggs and dairy allows us to embrace luxury and decadence.

Eggs and dairy products each separately harness a rich flavor profile; when these two simple ingredients come together with heat they create something marvelous: Custards. The heat cooks the proteins in both the dairy and eggs, and as the mixture cools, the cooked proteins mature and set with the supple, rich body that we associate with custard. In my world, custards are just plain tasty. This simple combination paves the way to a long list of pastry components: sauces, pastry creams, ice creams, and Bavarians, to name a few.

I think we all agree that often the simplest and most basic of desserts are the most satisfying. I, for one, cannot eat enough ice cream. For that matter, I can't eat enough of anything with a rich, velvety, custardy texture. When you consider that custards are basically a combination of milk, eggs, cream, and sugar, you realize that it takes really great ingredients to make a custard taste luscious and spot-on.

When I worked in New York City, I was called a tree hugger because of my obsession with locally sourced, organic ingredients. Upon my return to California, I've realized that I really am a tree hugger, and I am quite proud of it. Living in San Francisco, I have the opportunity not only to see and use great farmed products, but also to visit the source; and once I'm there, at the farm or the orchard, I realize why well-nurtured ingredients taste so amazing. They are produced and grown with love, in the same way that, every day, my staff and I produce our pastries and treats with love and caring attention.

the egg—where it all began

While they may be stored in the dairy section of the grocery store, and even the smallest dairy farm often sells eggs along with its milk, cheese, and cream, let's not forget that eggs are not a dairy product, meaning that they don't come from cows. Eggs are a protein-filled, inexpensive gift from chickens and other bird friends. Each ingenious shell contains fats, proteins, and vitamins. They thicken dough, when whipped up they lift desserts to airy new heights, and, most important, they bind together with milk and cream to create custards. Eggs are a symbol of fertility, new beginnings, and springtime. They've been used in food all over the world for centuries, and because of this we know a lot about the ways they react with cold and heat, whether whipped or cracked directly over a steaming bowl of egg drop soup.

I use and encourage you to buy local and organic, and this is definitely ideal for eggs. In the United States, there is very little oversight regarding how long eggs have sat on the store shelf or in the shipping warehouse. Most chickens in mass production are treated with little regard to life and are fed low-grade grain. Their living conditions affect the eggs that eventually end up on our kitchen tables.

As a Buddhist, I strive to pay attention to the system of life and how I affect it in my choices each day. Chickens deserve to be happy, just as cows, dogs, unicorns, and people do. Even if you don't always have the luxury of buying eggs from a small local farmer, you can still get cage-free and organic eggs in most supermarkets, a purchase that will pay for itself in flavor and health.

Two of my closest friends, Ken and Danny, recently moved farther away from the city and built a chicken coop in their new backyard. Living in their chicken coop, the Cluck Mahal, are ten colorful, fluffy, chirping hens and one tiny rooster named Froghorn Leghorn. To ensure companionship, they have at least two of each breed, and each chicken has a name. There are the golden girls, from the Orpington breed—Dorothy, Blanche, Sophia, and Rose—as well as my favorites, the white, fluffy Silkie couple, Björk and Dot. Aside from my dog, Maui, and their dog, Copper, causing a hilarious riot by the coop every time I visit them, these chickens live a happy and well-fed life. Sadly, the number of eggs they produce is too few for me to cook with at Tout Sweet, but they have contributed to many delicious brunches and inspired my already active love and obsession with the egg as an ingredient and a star player in a dish.

In pastry, the question is not which came first, the chicken or the egg, but which to use, the yolk or the white. Egg whites are almost completely free of fat and are made up mostly of water. They can be whipped up into stiff, magical peaks. I'll talk more later about French, Italian, and Swiss meringue; for now let me just say that egg whites are extremely temperamental, and the secret to a good meringue is a clean egg white (no yolk at all) and a clean, dry bowl (no flour dust, water, or other bits) at the start. Yolks are mostly fat and protein, bringing a special richness and body to any dessert, especially sauces. They also contain lecithin, a well-known emulsifier. This means that when a yolk is beaten with oil and vinegar, the molecules separate and then come together in a creamy, lovely dressing. A hollandaise sauce gets its creamy lusciousness from the egg yolk beaten into submission and emulsified with clarified butter. Yum!

dairy—milk, cream, cheese, and the happiness of a cow

I am lucky enough to live and work in the San Francisco Bay Area, where the local movement is moving and shaking everything in our food culture. Any Saturday morning that I can, I spend at the Ferry Plaza Farmers Market, perusing the stalls for new and needed ingredients. I always make a stop at the dairy stalls. Cheesemongers (those who have dedicated their lives to the love and details of cheese) are brilliant people who have found their passion. After spending 15 minutes speaking with a great cheesemonger, I feel a little silly and realize how much I still have to learn about their world. Even if you live far from a city or a farmers' market, chat up the manager in your grocery store's dairy aisle or meet the owners of local specialty stores. Searching out the best local cheese, milk, and cream will add to your knowledge of the ingredients and improve the local system of farming in your area. It will also mean a more flavorful, to-die-for dessert on your table.

Since Louis Pasteur invented pasteurization, a method of preservation that involves increasing the temperature of the milk for a few minutes and then reducing it back down, we've been able to store and ship milk and cream products over longer distances and have been able to keep them refrigerated over longer periods of time before they spoil. But this process does affect the flavor, so aim for milk that has been handled as little as possible. I realize that sometimes it's difficult to justify buying very expensive ingredients at natural markets, but milk is one place where the difference in flavor speaks loudly.

Fresh cow's milk is made up of casein, which makes the thick curds that end up as cheese, and whey, the thin green liquid that separates from the curds.

Fresh, full-cream milk that is left to sit will eventually separate into cream and milk. Light cream contains 18 to 30 percent fat, and heavy cream (what we whip into whipped cream and chantilly) contains 36 to 48 percent fat. Whole milk contains 3.2 percent fat and, unless otherwise specified, is what I am referring to in the recipes in this book when milk is called for.

Milk is completely affected by its environment: the temperature, the yeast in the air, moisture, and the time that it has sat idle. A cheese from the Swiss Alps is going to have many different notes than one from the rolling hills of the Bay Area. The environment affects not only the flavors, but also how the milk will act in cooked dishes. This is one of the reasons why I insist on local, organic milk products. When we heat milk to boiling or work with it directly from the refrigerator, we are working with it in two completely different forms. The natural makeup of milk means that heat breaks it down and then realigns its molecules. When a recipe calls for milk at room temperature, make sure to give it time to warm up before you start working with it.

Milk is just the beginning of myriad cheeses. Cheesemakers begin with milk, separate it into casein and whey with an acid, add rennet, and then do their magic. They control the time and temperature of the environment that it sits in, apply pressure and other techniques to the molded milk solids, and voilà! We have a soft, creamy cheese, or a hard, crumbly cheese, or something in the middle. Over the centuries, countless lives have been dedicated to creating and perfecting cheeses, and many books have been written on the topic, so I'll just say that great cheese can awaken your tongue, the back of your throat, and the roof of

your mouth in a way that is both complex and astronomical. Good cheese carries not only a supple mouthfeel but a tangy and complex flavor. And in my line of work, the perfect cheese plate served with dessert is an incredible treat for the palate. It balances the sweetness and brings out flavors that otherwise might go unnoticed.

Several years ago, I was lucky enough to be invited to one of the local dairies in Petaluma, about 30 minutes north of San Francisco. My friend Maureen, a cheesemonger, arranged a trip for a few of us to visit the dairy and a local cheesemaker to increase our understanding of their direct relationship. After spending a few minutes at the dairy, I was smiling from ear to ear. As they took us around the farm, showing us their various methods of milking and feeding, there was a loud, raucous, yet joyful jingling sound of cowbells. Yes, cowbells made my heart sing! The cows give an average 8 gallons (30 L) of milk per day, and they get milked twice a day. And these cows were happy. Their milk tasted delicious, and the cheese! Deep, tart, rich, tangy—the reason that cheese persists as a favorite way to start or end a meal.

That day on the farm I also realized how different a glass of milk can taste at different times in its life. Of course, this difference is going to affect the flavors of a milk-based food. Both a chantilly and a custard rely on the creamy goodness of cow's milk, and their flavor will change dramatically if they start with a fresh, organic cream. If you are going to take the time to make a beautiful dessert, take the time to find the freshest ingredients you can. Fresh milk is a simple way to take this first step.

meringue

A basic meringue consists of egg whites whipped, with the introduction of sugar, until the mixture reaches frothy, ribboning firm peaks. The temperature of the sugar is what creates different varieties of meringues. French meringues lend themselves to soufflés, and when folded create light and delicate cakes such as the classic *dacquoise* or my flourless chocolate cake. Some desserts cross between worlds; for example, some chefs prefer French meringue in creating French macarons, and some prefer an Italian meringue. While I believe there are right and wrong ways of preparing most desserts, I do recognize that there are also factors that are a matter of preference and taste.

FRENCH MERINGUE. A French meringue is simply egg whites whipped up to stand in firm peaks, with granulated sugar added after the egg whites have begun to take on air. You might call this the no-bake of meringues, as no heat is added during the process of whipping. This makes it simple, but it also makes it the least stable of meringues. When working with a French meringue, always make sure your egg whites are at room temperature; if they are not, you won't obtain full volume. Also, adding a small amount of acid to the egg whites prior to whipping will help stabilize your meringue, furthering your chances for success. You can do this by adding ½ teaspoon cream of tartar or a few tablespoons of lemon juice. Most soufflés have a French meringue folded into the batter before baking, to give the soufflé its famous, gravity-defying lift. When working with French meringues, there is a good chance the egg whites will deflate if they sit too long or are handled roughly. To avoid this, whip your eggs and sugar just before you add the meringue to the batter and fold it into the batter with a rubber spatula in thirds. Do not add the entire meringue to the batter at once.

Another very important factor in creating a great French meringue is knowing when to introduce the sugar. Although it's a common practice, it's not a good idea to begin adding the sugar when you first start to whip the egg whites. If introduced too early, the sugar will in fact start to pull the water out of the egg whites, deflating the final mix. I like to whip my egg whites on medium speed, creating small, frothy bubbles that are more stable and stronger in their bonds. When the egg whites form soft, glossy peaks, start to sprinkle the sugar in, slowly and continuously, until it is all incorporated into the meringue. Once all the sugar is added, mix the meringue for an additional 2 minutes or so, to ensure that the sugar has dissolved into the whites, creating medium-firm peaks. French meringue is called for in the mirliton cake on page 101.

ITALIAN MERINGUE. The Italian meringue has a cooked sugar and sometimes an invert sugar to stabilize it and help avoid crystallization. This requires cooking a sugar syrup to 249°F (121°C) and then adding it slowly to the whipped egg whites, with the mixer still mixing on medium-high speed. Most recipes will direct you to pour the sugar along the edge of the bowl—follow this advice! Pouring the hot sugar directly into the egg whites will deflate them and quite possibly cook them. Use the side of the bowl as a conductor and as a way to control the speed at which the sugar is added to the meringue. The heat of the sugar will help stabilize the meringue by "maturing" the protein in the egg whites as they are whipped together. Remember that you are going to continue to whip your egg whites as you add the sugar, so I like to time it so that I have the egg whites at soft peaks just as the sugar is reaching 249°F (121°C). That way, the hot sugar is pouring in as the egg whites finish whipping. Believe me, overwhipped egg whites can result in a hot, sticky mess!

SWISS MERINGUE. The Swiss have the most stable meringue. This meringue is cooked over a bain-marie as it is whipped to firm peaks. The meringue is started over hot, simmering water, brought to about 130°F (55°C), and then finished away from the heat. A thermometer is extremely useful here, but you do have a window of a few degrees. The heat is not meant to cook the egg whites; it is meant to denature, or mature, them. This means that the protein will change and become more stable in the airy mixture but will not turn the eggs into a scrambled mess— egg white omelets, anyone? As you whisk your egg whites, take them away from the simmering water every 30 seconds so that the bowl doesn't get too hot. They will foam and then take on an extra shine. The outside of the bowl should be warm but never hot, and the eggs should feel warm to the touch. When the mixture reaches 130°F (55°C), remove the bowl from the heat completely and whip the meringue to a glossy, silky, firm-peaked masterpiece. This can be done from start to finish in the metal bowl of a stand mixer. You'll use this method in my Baked Berry Meringue Kisses recipe on 78.

All meringues take a certain amount of careful handling. But they bring an airy lift, a beautiful body, and some extra style to the dessert world. And they don't have to be white; a few drops of food coloring, some delicate flavoring, and an oven on low heat, and you've got a beautiful, melt-in-your-mouth treat. Mastering meringues opens a new world of recipes and ways to be creative with your desserts. Trust me—taking the time to learn to work with the magical egg white is worth it.

french lavender pavlovas

The Pavlova was made to honor Russian ballerina Anna Pavlova in the 1920s. Remember that when you're working with this recipe. It should be as light, airy, and poetic as a captivating, well-rehearsed, and well-executed ballet. The colors and the flavors in this rendition are much more modern than the classic. If the original was created for a Russian ballerina, this version might be for Martha Graham's modern dance company. This recipe can be a little painstaking to perfect, but do try it. It's worth all the effort.

YIELD: 150 PAVLOVAS

---

150 g/5 egg whites

5 g/1 tsp white distilled vinegar (optional)

6 to 8 drops purple food coloring (optional)

1 drop black food coloring (optional)

70 g/¹/₃ cup plus heaping 2 tsp granulated sugar, plus 200 g/1 cup

40 g/¹/₃ cup cornstarch

15 g/1 tbsp lemon juice

3 or 4 drops culinary lavender oil

Set the egg whites on the counter for 1 to 2 hours so that they are at room temperature when you work with them. Preheat the oven to 175°F (80°C). If you choose to use the food coloring, in a small bowl, combine the vinegar with the purple and black food coloring. Set aside. Line a baking sheet with parchment paper.

In a small bowl, combine the 70 g/¹/₃ cup plus heaping 2 tsp sugar with the cornstarch, using a whisk or clean fingertips to mix them together.

In the bowl of a stand mixer fitted with the whisk attachment, add the lemon juice to the egg whites. Whisk the egg whites to soft peaks, as if making a French meringue (see page 74).

When the egg whites have tripled in size and are light and foamy, slowly add the remaining 200 g/1 cup sugar, whisking until evenly mixed. Increase the mixer speed to medium-high and whisk until the egg whites rise another 50 percent in volume and take on a light, glossy, firm texture. When the meringue has reached beautiful, firm peaks, reduce the mixer speed to medium-low and then add the sugar-cornstarch mixture. Whisk for another 30 seconds to evenly combine. Add the culinary lavender oil and, if using, gently pour in the food coloring mixture. Whisk on medium speed for 5 seconds, or until evenly combined.

Turn off the mixer and remove the bowl of glossy meringue from the stand. Fit a piping bag with a #4 round piping tip and use a rubber spatula to load the meringue into the piping bag until it's half full. Remove the parchment paper from the baking sheet and pipe a small dollop of meringue directly onto each corner of the baking sheet; place the parchment paper back onto the baking sheet and press down on the corners. This will hold the paper down during baking. Hold the piping bag upright and pipe $1^1/_2$-in (4-cm) rounds while moving the piping bag in an upward motion. Leave 1 in (2.5 cm) between the dollops of meringue.

Dip a clean spoon into hot water, shake off the excess and then, with the back of the spoon, create a divot in the center of each meringue round. Each meringue should look like two sloping hills with a valley in the middle. Clean the spoon well and dip it again into the hot water after every two or three meringues so that there is no meringue sticking to the spoon. Place the sheet of meringues into the oven and bake for 1 hour, rotate the baking sheet 180 degrees, and bake for another 45 minutes.

To check doneness, pull one meringue off the parchment paper. It should pull off cleanly. If the meringues need more time, return the baking sheet to the oven and keep checking at 15-minute intervals until they come off the baking sheet easily and cleanly. After they've been baked, the Pavlovas can be stored in an airtight container in a cool, dry place for up to 1 week.

baked berry meringue kisses

Warning: These meringue kisses are absolutely adorable. When we bake multiple trays of them in the kitchen, they look like a uniform, sweet army, all standing at attention, ready to capture desserts and hearts. They often outshine the confections they sit on top of and are a great way of drawing attention to your creations. Small, shiny, sweet treats really tap into your inner child. The beauty of these meringue kisses is that they are so simple to make, and you can adjust their flavor and color to suit your taste. I've also made them with passion fruit and lime, strawberry and vanilla, and Ceylon cinnamon. But don't let me get in the way of your creative process!

YIELD: 200 KISSES

---

10 g/2 tbsp freeze-dried raspberries or other berry

90 g/3 egg whites

210 g/1¾ cups plus 1 tbsp powdered sugar

3 drops red food coloring

Red sanding sugar for sprinkling

Use a food processor to pulverize the freeze-dried raspberries to a sandy texture. Sift the pulverized raspberries through a fine-mesh sieve into a bowl and set aside. Line a baking sheet with parchment paper. Preheat the oven to 150°F (65°C).

Bring a large saucepan of water to a boil. Wipe out the heatproof bowl of a stand mixer with a clean towel, and then combine the egg whites and powdered sugar in the bowl. Turn down the boiling water to a simmer, and place the mixing bowl over the saucepan to create a bain-marie. Use a handheld wire whisk to stir the egg white and sugar mixture over the heat until the sugar dissolves and the egg whites are warm to the touch, approximately 122°F (50°C). The mixture will look full and glossy, like a marshmallow sauce. Wipe the outside of the bowl dry and move it to the stand mixer fitted with the whisk attachment. Continue whisking the egg white mixture at high speed until stiff, glossy peaks form, cooling it to approximately 77°F (25°C). Add the ground and sifted freeze-dried raspberry powder and food coloring and continue to whisk for 1 minute more. It's important to add the fruit powder at the very end, after the meringue has cooled; otherwise the

CONTINUED . . .

powder will absorb the moisture in the warm meringue, causing the final product to be soggy and chewy.

Use a rubber spatula to load the raspberry meringue into a piping bag fitted with a #3 round piping tip. Before starting, remove the parchment paper from the baking sheet and pipe a small dollop of meringue directly onto each corner of the baking sheet; place the parchment paper back onto the baking sheet and press down on the corners. This will hold the paper down during baking. To create the kisses, use an upward motion to pipe the meringue in $1/4$-in- (6-mm-) diameter rounds onto the baking sheet. They will be shiny and light red. Pipe them in lines down the baking sheet, with just enough space between them to allow air circulation, about $1/4$ in (6 mm). Sprinkle the kisses immediately with sanding sugar and shake the pan lightly in your hand, ensuring that all the sugar sticks to the kisses.

Bake for 1 hour, rotate the baking sheet 180 degrees, and bake for another hour. To check doneness, pull one meringue kiss off the baking sheet. It should pull off easily and cleanly and once cooled to room temperature should be crisp and melt on your tongue. If the kiss sticks to the paper or is still soft to the bite, return the baking sheet to the oven and keep checking at 15-minute intervals until done.

Serve immediately. (Do not refrigerate.)

explore your chantilly

Chantilly is the French word for whipped cream and usually indicates that there are ingredients besides cream in the airy, whipped-up masterpiece on your plate. No matter what you call it, it's a good thing. Have you ever made freshly whipped cream at a dinner party? I encourage you to do so. I'm still tickled when people get excited and, with delight glowing on their faces, ask, "Is that fresh whipped cream?" Chantilly is a basic component of fillings, creams, and many classic—and not-so-classic—desserts. I've included four variations of chantilly here. Each has a different flavor profile, but the method is the same, and absurdly simple.

The basic steps for chantilly are as follows:

1. Combine all the room-temperature ingredients in a large bowl or the bowl of a stand mixer.

2. Use a large, balloon-shaped whisk or the whisk attachment to whip the ingredients to full peak stage; do not overwhip (we're not making butter here, folks).

3. Serve immediately.

vanilla bean chantilly

This is the classic chantilly, or whipped cream, recipe that we all know and love. Serve it on a Dark Chocolate Crémeux (page 161) or on top of hot chocolate, or just sneak spoonfuls from the refrigerator. Once you become comfortable with this recipe, you can begin to add ingredients to create your own flavor profiles.

YIELD: ABOUT 2 CUPS (480 ML)

250 g/1 cup plus
1 tbsp heavy cream

40 g/3 tbsp granulated sugar

Seeds of $\frac{1}{2}$ vanilla bean or
4 g/1 tsp vanilla bean paste
(see Sources, page 216)

CONTINUED . . .

crème fraîche chantilly

The tartness of the crème fraîche and the deep sweetness of the honey balance this chantilly to make a well-rounded, creamy treat. The crème fraîche will increase the time and the muscle required to get to the full peak stage, but I promise it is worth the effort. **YIELD: ABOUT 2 CUPS (480 ML)**

250 g/1 cup plus 1 tbsp crème fraîche

250 g/1 cup plus 1 tbsp heavy cream

30 g/1½ tbsp lavender honey

Grated zest of ¼ orange (see page 110)

---

rose water chantilly

Rose water is a common ingredient in Mediterranean cuisine; it has a beautiful fragrance and adds a special something when used in the correct amount. The flavors in this recipe are rounded out by the rose water and crème fraîche. This is the perfect complement to spring and summer fruit desserts. **YIELD: ABOUT 2 CUPS (480 ML)**

200 g/¾ cup plus 1 tbsp heavy cream

50 g/3 tbsp crème fraîche

20 g/1 tbsp plus 1 tsp rose water

30 g/2 tbsp plus heaping 1 tsp granulated sugar

---

mascarpone chantilly

We were working on a stuffing for French toast and hit upon this as a complement and balance to the rich sweetness of the classic brunch treat. It is also a great topping for hot toddies at the end of a wintry Saturday. The cognac and the creaminess of the mascarpone bring whipped cream to the adult table. **YIELD: ABOUT 4 CUPS (960 ML)**

150 g/⅔ cup mascarpone

120 g/½ cup heavy cream

15 g/heaping 1 tbsp granulated sugar

2 tsp cognac

Grated zest of ¼ orange (see page 110)

20 g/1 tbsp orange marmalade

citrus-scented panna cotta

Panna cotta is an Italian delight with a creamy, soft feel in the mouth. Its texture shouldn't be bouncy; rather, it should hold its form when spooned just so. Once the spoon makes it into your mouth, the panna cotta should gently melt. This is a simple recipe that can make 5 or 50 desserts, quickly and in advance.

I like to say this is citrus "scented" because that's exactly how the citrus imparts flavor into the custard. The fruity tartness of the citrus is the perfect pairing for the rich flavor of the cream; but when mixed together, citrus juice and cream tend to curdle. By infusing the flavors of orange and lemon zests into the body of the cream, you get a delightful, delicate flavor profile that is truly simple and elegant. I imagine that if I had an Italian grandmother, this is the sort of dessert she would approve of. **YIELD: 3¹/₂ CUPS (1 KG)**

---

700 g/3 cups heavy cream	**150 g/³/₄ cup granulated sugar**
Grated zest of 1 orange (see page 110)	**30 g/3 tbsp plus 1 tsp powdered gelatin or 10 gelatin leaves**
Grated zest of 1 lemon (see page 110)	**140 g/¹/₂ cup plus 1 tbsp buttermilk**
1 vanilla bean or 12 g/1 tbsp vanilla bean paste (see Sources, page 216)	

In a medium stainless-steel or enamel-coated saucepan, bring 350 g/1¹/₂ cups of the heavy cream to a boil over medium-high heat; reserve the other half in the refrigerator to keep it cold. Remove the saucepan from the heat and add the orange zest and lemon zest to the hot cream. Split the vanilla bean in half lengthwise with a paring knife and then use the knife to scrape the seeds from the pod. Add the seeds and pod or the vanilla bean paste to the hot cream. Whisk everything together and cover the saucepan, allowing the vanilla bean and citrus zests to infuse into the cream for 1 hour.

Remove the vanilla pod and return the cream infusion to the stovetop over medium-high heat. Add the sugar and bring the cream back to a boil, stirring occasionally with a rubber spatula and scraping the bottom so that the cream does not burn.

Meanwhile, if using powdered gelatin, sprinkle it over a small saucepan containing $1/3$ cup (75 ml) water and allow to sit for 5 minutes to hydrate the gelatin. Place over medium-low heat for another 5 minutes to completely dissolve the gelatin into the water. If using gelatin leaves, bloom them by placing them in a clean bowl of cold water for 5 minutes, then drain and squeeze out all excess water. Add the gelatin-water or bloomed gelatin to the hot cream mixture and whisk until the gelatin dissolves.

Pour the reserved 350 g/$1^{1}/_{2}$ cups cold heavy cream into the saucepan and whisk to combine (cooling the cream down will keep the butter-milk from separating when it is added). Add the buttermilk to the cooled cream mixture and whisk to combine thoroughly.

Pour the panna cotta into your desired glass-ware or dish and refrigerate for a minimum of 3 hours, allowing it to set to a beautiful soft, jiggly texture. You can pour the panna cottas up to 5 days before serving. If not serving imme-diately, cover the tops with plastic wrap so they do not dry out.

ricotta-mascarpone filling with cognac

One day a client asked me to make cannoli. I have to admit, having worked mainly in French kitchens, and having seen and tasted many bad cannoli, I had never attempted to create my own. When faced with the request, I became a deer in the headlights. So I put the task into the hands of my friend Carol, my sous chef at the time. She is well versed in Mediterranean cooking, and I never shy away from asking someone who knows a recipe better than I do to show me the way. What I fell in love with wasn't the fried shell but her take on the cream filling. It's simply divine. Since then, I've used variations of it in many applications. Thanks, Carol! **YIELD: 3¹/₂ CUPS (840 ML)**

**185 g/³/₄ cup
Spring Hill small curd ricotta cheese**

**130 g/¹/₂ cup plus 1 tbsp
mascarpone cheese**

30 g/2¹/₂ tbsp granulated sugar

Grated zest of 1 orange (see page 110)

15 g/1 tbsp vanilla cognac

10 g/1¹/₂ tsp orange flower water

5 g/³/₄ tsp kosher salt

240 g/1 cup heavy cream

About 1 hour before you plan to make the filling, place the ricotta and mascarpone on the counter so that they come to room temperature.

In a stand mixer fitted with the paddle attachment, combine both cheeses, the sugar, orange zest, cognac, orange flower water, and salt. Mix on low speed for about 20 seconds, or until just evenly combined. Switch to the whisk attachment, using a rubber spatula to clean the paddle into the mixer bowl. Set the mixer on medium speed and add the heavy cream, whisking until the mixture becomes a lighter, whipped cream. Take care not to overwhip, so you don't break the mascarpone and the heavy cream. The final mixture should have a creamy, spoonable texture. This mixture will keep stored in an airtight container in the refrigerator, for up to 5 days.

Sweet Note: This filling works beautifully as a base for most fruit tarts. Pipe a thin layer inside your baked tart shell and top it with sweet blueberries and slices of juicy nectarines, or port-glazed figs.

vanilla bean pastry cream

When I was a kid, my aunt would make fresh pastry cream, layer it over strawberries, and give it to me as an after-dinner treat. I loved the way it filled my mouth with silky, rich vanilla sweetness and brought extra notes to the strawberries. To this day I have an intense love of a great French éclair filled with the luscious custard.

If there were a class called Pastry 101, a great pastry cream would certainly be one of the first lessons, and I am grateful for my early introduction to the recipe. In the kitchen it's as essential to a pastry chef's repertoire as a good tart dough, acting as a base for filling a variety of creations, from cream puffs to wedding cakes. **YIELD: 4 CUPS (960 ML)**

---

510 g/2 cups whole milk

$\frac{1}{2}$ **vanilla bean or 10 g/2 tsp vanilla bean paste (see Sources, page 216)**

115 g/$\frac{1}{2}$ cup plus 1 tbsp granulated sugar

140 g/7 egg yolks

35 g/$\frac{1}{4}$ cup cornstarch

60 g/$\frac{1}{4}$ cup unsalted butter, cut into $\frac{1}{2}$-in (12-mm) cubes, at room temperature

---

Place a fine-mesh strainer over a medium bowl.

Pour the milk into a medium stainless-steel or enamel-coated saucepan. Split the vanilla bean in half lengthwise with a paring knife and then use the knife to scrape the seeds from the pod. Add the seeds and pod or the vanilla bean paste to the milk. Whisk the mixture together and bring to a boil over medium heat. Cover the saucepan, remove from the heat, and allow the vanilla to infuse into the milk for 1 hour. Meanwhile, combine the sugar, egg yolks, and cornstarch in a separate medium bowl and whisk together until smooth.

Return the saucepan of milk and vanilla to the stovetop and bring to a boil over medium heat. Add some of the hot milk mixture to the sugar-egg mixture, $\frac{1}{4}$ cup (60 ml) at a time, until the contents of the bowl are warm to the touch. This will temper the eggs so that they will not scramble when cooking. Add the contents of the bowl to the saucepan. Use a whisk to stir the mixture over medium heat while it returns to a boil. Boil for 1 to 2 minutes. When the first large bubble appears, whisk for another 30 to 45 seconds, until the mixture is glossy, light yellow, and beginning to noticeably thicken.

Remove the saucepan from the heat. Strain the thickened custard through the prepared fine-mesh strainer into the clean bowl, removing the vanilla pod and ensuring that there are no lumps in the final custard. Cover with plastic wrap, placing it directly on top of the custard to prevent a skin from forming, and allow it to cool to a temperature between 95° and 104°F (35° and 40°C). Alternatively, place the bowl over an ice bath to cool.

Add the room-temperature butter cubes to the custard and use a handheld blender to emulsify the butter into the custard. Place plastic wrap directly on top of the custard and set it in the refrigerator for 2 to 3 hours, or overnight. Once cooled, the pastry cream can be stored in an airtight container in the refrigerator up to 7 days.

Sweet Note: For a simple way to enjoy pastry cream, try serving it in small bowls sprinkled with fresh berries or slices of stone fruit. It can also be used as a base for fruit tarts or layered between crispy caramelized puff pastry. It is also pure perfection on its own.

orange flower water diplomat cream

This is a simple follow-up to the Vanilla Bean Pastry Cream. The addition of orange flower water makes this filling appropriate for a sophisticated crowd and wonderful for filling cakes and other pastries such as the layered crêpe cake (page 202). **YIELD: 6 CUPS (1.4 L)**

---

1 recipe Vanilla Bean Pastry Cream (page 88)

12 g/1 tbsp plus 1 tsp powdered gelatin or 4 silver gelatin leaves

670 g/2³/₄ cups plus 3 tbsp heavy cream

25 g/1 tbsp plus 2 tsp orange flower water

Grated zest of 1 orange (see page 110)

Place the pastry cream in a medium bowl on the counter to come to room temperature. It is at the perfect temperature for this recipe just after the butter has been added and emulsified. If it's too cold, the gelatin will not distribute evenly, creating lumps in the mixture.

If using powdered gelatin, sprinkle it over a small saucepan containing ¹/₄ cup (60 ml) water and allow it to sit for 5 minutes to hydrate the gelatin. Place over medium heat and whisk to fully dissolve the gelatin into the water. If using gelatin leaves, bloom them by placing them in a clean bowl of cold water for 5 minutes, then drain and squeeze out all excess water. Meanwhile, in a stand mixer fitted with the whisk attachment, whip the heavy cream to medium-firm peaks. Set aside in the refrigerator.

Pour the orange flower water into a separate medium glass or plastic bowl. Add the gelatin-water or bloomed gelatin to the orange flower water. Microwave this mixture for 20 to 30 seconds, until the gelatin is completely melted and is warm. Remove from the microwave and stir to combine. If not using a microwave, heat the gelatin–orange flower water mixture in a small saucepan over low heat for 1 minute, or until the gelatin is completely melted and the mixture is warm.

Use a rubber spatula to scrape the orange flower gelatin and the orange zest into the pastry cream and whisk to distribute the gelatin. Finally, using a rubber spatula, gently fold the cold whipped cream into the pastry cream mixture; this will create a soft, mousselike texture. The diplomat cream is now ready to use.

Sweet Note: The key to using diplomat cream is timing. Once it is finished, it will be soft enough to spread onto cake layers, but it will quickly start to set. So be sure you have all your other components handy and ready to assemble.

tahitian vanilla bean ice cream

If ice cream is a thing worth screaming for, then for its most simple, perfectly flavored form—vanilla—we should all be losing our voices. After all, vanilla ice cream is to sundaes as a stretched canvas is to an artist. When working with this recipe, you absolutely must not cut corners. Purchase good vanilla beans. Otherwise, there are so many acceptable forms of ice cream on the grocery shelf that it is not worth your time to make it. **YIELD: 8 CUPS (2 L)**

1.2 kg/5¼ cups whole milk

120 g/½ cup heavy cream

1 vanilla bean or 12 g/1 tbsp vanilla bean paste (see Sources, page 216)

300 g/15 egg yolks

275 g/1⅓ cups plus scant 1 tbsp granulated sugar

In a medium stainless-steel or enamel-coated saucepan, combine the milk and heavy cream; bring to a boil over medium heat. While heating the milk mixture, split the vanilla bean in half lengthwise with a paring knife and then use the knife to scrape the seeds out from the pod. Add both the seeds and the pod or the vanilla bean paste to the saucepan; whisk to combine. Remove from the heat. Cover the saucepan of hot milk and vanilla; set aside for 1 to 2 hours to create a rich infusion.

Add ice to a large bowl, filling it just over halfway, and then add cold water to almost cover the ice. Set out a medium bowl that will fit into the ice-water bowl. Make sure the water won't spill out when the smaller bowl is placed into the ice bath. Have a fine-mesh sieve handy.

In a separate medium bowl, combine the egg yolks and sugar. Whisk to break up the yolks and combine them with the sugar. Return the milk infusion to the stove and bring it back to a boil over medium heat. Temper the egg yolks by adding ½ cup (120 ml) of the hot milk to the egg yolk mixture and whisking to combine. This method will keep the egg yolks from cooking when you add them to the hot milk.

Slowly add the tempered egg mixture to the milk, whisking the milk mixture constantly as you pour it in. Once the egg yolk mixture is fully incorporated, continue cooking it over medium heat, stirring continuously with a rubber spatula so that the mixture does not stick to the bottom of the saucepan. Use the rubber spatula to keep the sides of the saucepan clean. Cook the mixture until it reaches 180°F (82°C).

Strain the custard through the prepared fine-mesh sieve into the medium bowl, removing the vanilla pod and any undesired lumps that may have formed during cooking. Place the bowl of custard into the ice bath and chill it to room temperature. Cover and chill the strained custard in the refrigerator overnight until it "matures," or reaches about 40°F (4°C). The next day, freeze the custard in an ice-cream maker according to the manufacturer's instructions.

Sweet Note: Time strengthens the bonds between egg yolk proteins to create a silky-smooth ice cream without chunks or ice crystals. An overnight rest for the custard will greatly improve the final ice cream.

cherry-vanilla ice cream

Colorful and fruity, this ice cream is a quick variation on the Tahitian Vanilla Bean Ice Cream (page 92). The cherry purée adds a pink-red color and a light, fruity tartness to the ice cream, making a great recipe better. In this recipe, I use Bing cherries for their rich flavor and color profile, but if you are lucky enough to have access to fresh sour cherries, by all means use them! They will lend a tangy complement to the sweet, creamy ice cream. **YIELD: 8 CUPS (2 L)**

---

640 g/2 cups plus 2 tsp Bing cherry purée

430 g/1³/₄ cups plus scant 1 tbsp whole milk

1 scant tbsp heavy cream

1 vanilla bean or 12 g/1 tbsp vanilla bean paste (see Sources, page 216)

1 star anise

160 g/8 egg yolks

150 g/³/₄ cup plus scant 1 tbsp granulated sugar

Place the cherry purée into a medium stainless-steel or enamel-coated saucepan and bring to a simmer over medium-low heat. Occasionally stir the purée with a heat-resistant rubber spatula, making sure the purée does not stick to the bottom of the saucepan and burn. Let simmer until reduced by half. Set aside.

In a separate, medium stainless-steel or enamel-coated saucepan, combine the milk and heavy cream; bring to a boil over medium-high heat. While heating the milk mixture, split the vanilla bean in half lengthwise with a paring knife, and then use the knife to scrape the seeds from the pod. Add both the seeds and the pod or the vanilla bean paste to the saucepan, along with the star anise, and whisk to combine. Remove from the heat. Cover and let rest for 1 to 2 hours to create a rich infusion.

Add ice to a large bowl, filling it just over half-way, and then add cold water to almost cover the ice. Set out a medium bowl that will fit into the ice-water bowl. Make sure the water won't spill out when the smaller bowl is placed into the ice bath. Have a fine-mesh sieve handy.

In a separate medium bowl, combine the egg yolks and sugar. Whisk to break up the yolks and combine them with the sugar. Return the milk infusion to the stove and bring it back to a boil over medium heat. Temper the egg yolks by adding ¹/₂ cup (120 ml) of the hot milk to the egg yolk mixture and whisking to combine. This method will keep the egg yolks from cooking when you add them to the hot milk.

Slowly add the tempered mixture to the milk, whisking the milk mixture constantly as you pour it in. Once the egg yolk mixture is fully incorporated, continue cooking it over medium heat, stirring continuously with a rubber spatula so that the mixture does not stick to the bottom of the saucepan. Use the rubber spatula to keep the sides of the saucepan clean. Cook the mixture until it reaches 180°F (82°C). Gently stir in the reserved cherry purée.

Strain the custard through the prepared fine-mesh sieve into the medium bowl, removing the vanilla pod, star anise, and any undesired lumps that may have formed during cooking. Place the bowl of custard into the ice bath and chill it to room temperature. Cover and chill the strained custard in the refrigerator overnight until it "matures," or reaches about 40°F (4°C). The next day, freeze the custard in an ice-cream maker according to the manufacturer's instructions.

lemongrass & ginger ice cream

Simplicity and complexity exist harmoniously in this ice cream. By ratio, this ice cream base has less egg yolk, allowing the final product to really present the delicate aromas of the lemongrass, ginger, and kaffir lime in a clean and clear way. These three flavors are used in many Asian cuisines, especially Thai, which has always been a favorite of mine. If eaten by itself, this ice cream has a more savory flair, but you'll find that it pairs beautifully with any fruit that harnesses sweetness and acidity together, such as berries and most stone fruits. **YIELD: 8 CUPS (2 L)**

---

845 g/3½ cups whole milk, plus more to replace after infusion

190 g/¾ cup plus scant 1 tbsp heavy cream

One 2-in (5-cm) stalk lemongrass

45 g/about a 4-in (10-cm) piece fresh ginger

1 kaffir lime leaf (optional)

80 g/4 egg yolks

250 g/2½ cups granulated sugar

In a medium stainless-steel or enamel-coated saucepan, bring the milk and cream to a boil over medium heat, then reduce the heat to low. While the milk is heating, prepare the lemongrass and ginger. Use a clean hammer or meat tenderizer to pound the lemongrass until cracked and flattened but still in one piece. This will break down the lemongrass and release essential oils. Cut it into ½-in (12-mm) chunks. Peel the ginger and cut into ½-in (12-mm) chunks.

When the milk comes to a boil, add the lemongrass, ginger, and kaffir lime leaf (if using) to the milk and whisk to combine. Remove from the heat. Cover and let rest for 1 to 2 hours to create a vibrant aromatic infusion. After 2 hours, strain the liquid through a sieve into a clean, medium saucepan. (In this recipe, I don't leave the flavor ingredients in the custard, because if they impart too much flavor, it has the potential to overpower the ice cream. The beauty of this ice cream is allowing the lemongrass, ginger, and kaffir lime leaf to lend a delicate flavor.) Once you have strained the milk, measure it and add more milk to bring it back to 590 g/2½ cups, as the lemongrass and ginger will absorb some of the liquid during the infusing process.

Add ice to a large bowl, filling it just over halfway, and then add cold water to almost cover the ice. Set out a medium bowl that will fit into the ice-water bowl. Make sure the water won't spill out when the smaller bowl is placed into the ice bath. Have a fine-mesh sieve handy.

In a separate medium bowl, combine the egg yolks and sugar. Whisk to break up the yolks and combine them with the sugar. Return the milk infusion to the stove and bring it back to a boil over medium heat. Temper the egg yolks by adding $1/2$ cup (120 ml) of the hot milk to the egg yolk mixture and whisking to combine. This method will keep the egg yolks from cooking when you add them to the hot milk.

Slowly add the tempered mixture to the milk, whisking the milk mixture constantly as you pour it in. Once the egg yolk mixture is fully incorporated, continue cooking it over medium heat, stirring continuously with a rubber spatula so that the mixture does not stick to the bottom of the saucepan. Use the rubber spatula to keep the sides of the saucepan clean. Cook the mixture until it reaches 180°F (82°C). Strain the custard through the prepared fine-mesh sieve into the medium bowl. Place the bowl of custard into the ice bath and chill it to room temperature. Cover and chill the strained custard in the refrigerator overnight until it "matures," or reaches about 40°F (4°C). The next day, freeze the custard in an ice-cream maker according to the manufacturer's instructions.

burnt caramel ice cream

It's all in the name. As is suggested by the term *burnt*, this ice cream achieves its special hints of smokiness and depth when you push the caramelization process just beyond where you think you should stop. The "burning" of the caramel will add layers of flavor to this cold treat. Do pay attention, though. If it's too burnt, it may bring the dish to ruin. After all, you want to end on a sweet note, not a bitter one. **YIELD: 8 CUPS (2 L)**

120 g/$^1/_2$ cup heavy cream

90 g/$^1/_3$ cup plus scant 1 tbsp unsalted butter

200 g/1 cup granulated sugar, plus 50 g/$^1/_4$ cup

60 g/$^1/_4$ cup water

140 g/$^1/_3$ cup plus scant 2 tbsp light corn syrup

1.2 kg/4$^3/_4$ cups plus 1 tbsp whole milk

180 g/9 egg yolks

In a small stainless-steel or enamel-coated saucepan, combine the heavy cream and butter. Bring to a boil. Keep warm until ready for use.

In a separate 4- to 6-qt (3.8- to 5.7-L) stainless-steel or enamel-coated saucepan, combine the 200 g/1 cup sugar, water, and corn syrup. Use your fingers to mix them together. Cover the saucepan and bring the mixture to a boil over high heat. When it begins to boil, wait for 1 minute and then remove the lid. Heat the sugar syrup until it is a dark amber color and starts to smoke lightly; 392°F (200°C; see page 26).

Remove the cooked sugar syrup from the heat. Immediately whisk in a third of the warm, reserved cream–butter mixture. Take caution—hot steam will come up from the saucepan as you do this. Pour in the remainder of the cream mixture slowly while whisking continuously to obtain a smooth, rich caramel. Pour the milk

into the caramel and bring the mixture back to a boil, creating a liquid, milky caramel.

In a medium bowl, whisk together the egg yolks and the remaining 50 g/$^1/_4$ cup sugar. Temper the egg yolks by adding $^1/_2$ cup (120 ml) of the hot caramel mixture to the egg yolk mixture and whisking to combine. This method will keep the egg yolks from cooking when you add them to the hot caramel liquid.

Slowly add the tempered mixture to the caramel, whisking the caramel constantly as you pour it in. Once the egg yolk mixture is fully incorporated, continue cooking it over medium heat, stirring continuously with a rubber spatula so that the mixture does not stick to the bottom of the saucepan. Use the rubber spatula to keep the sides of the saucepan clean. Cook the mixture until it reaches 180°F (82°C).

Add ice to a large bowl, filling it just over halfway, and then add cold water to almost cover the ice. Set out a medium bowl that will fit into the ice-water bowl. Make sure the water won't spill out when the smaller bowl is placed into the ice bath. Have a fine-mesh sieve handy.

Strain the custard through the fine-mesh sieve into the medium bowl. Place the bowl of custard into the ice bath and chill it to room temperature. Cover and chill the strained custard in the refrigerator overnight until it "matures," or reaches about 40°F (4°C). The next day, freeze the custard in an ice-cream maker according to the manufacturer's instructions.

Sweet Note: Use a large saucepan for this recipe. Warm cream poured into caramelized sugar will expand more than you expect. Don't be afraid if the caramel smokes; in the end, it will add to the complexity of the flavor.

creamy mascarpone bavarian

This is similar to a classic French Bavarian with an Italian twist: the sweet mascarpone. It has a luscious mouthfeel and just the right amount of sweetness to balance the creamy texture of the mascarpone cheese. Unlike a traditional mousse, which uses gelatin, this dessert gets its texture from eggs that are cooked to a custard over a bain-marie and then whipped to fluffy peaks to encase the mascarpone and the heavy cream. Take care—mascarpone cheese is very delicate and doesn't like to be overhandled. This is a good test of your delicate pastry hands. **YIELD: 2 CUPS (480 ML)**

---

180 g/³/₄ cup mascarpone

180 g/³/₄ cup heavy cream

60 g/3 egg yolks

70 g/¹/₃ cup plus 2 tsp granulated sugar

20 g/1 tbsp plus 1 tsp water

Set the mascarpone out at least 1 hour before cooking so that it is fully at room temperature when you begin. Heat a saucepan of water to a simmer to create a bain-marie. In a large mixing bowl, whisk the heavy cream to medium peaks, or until a dollop pulled out of the bowl keeps its peak for 2 seconds and then begins to droop. Reserve at room temperature until ready for use.

Combine the egg yolks, sugar, and water in a medium stainless-steel bowl and place over the hot water. Whisk continuously until the mixture reaches 180°F (82°C). The mixture will take on a pale and thick consistency. Transfer the mixture to a stand mixer fitted with a whisk attachment and whip on high speed until the mixture reaches room temperature and has pale, stiff peaks.

In a separate medium bowl, use a rubber spatula to fold one-third of the whipped cream into the room-temperature mascarpone to lighten the mascarpone. Fold the lightened mascarpone into the egg yolk mixture and stir to evenly combine. Fold the remaining whipped cream into the mixture.

The Bavarian is best served immediately, but it can be reserved in the refrigerator for 1 day. Use a spoon or piping bag to divide it among serving dishes, or cover it with plastic wrap laid directly on the surface and chill until ready for use.

Sweet Note: This recipe is the perfect creamy, sweet, and tangy filling for a layer cake. To add more structure to the Bavarian, add 2 leaves bloomed gelatin, or 2 tsp gelatin powder dissolved in 1 tbsp warm water for 5 minutes, to the egg yolk mixture before you whisk them.

spiced hazelnut-almond mirliton cake

The mirliton is the easiest cake in my repertoire to prepare, as well as one of the tastiest. And as an added bonus, it is gluten-free. I chose to include this cake in the Eggs & Dairy chapter because it gets its structure from the wholesome goodness of eggs, with a little help from cornstarch. The almond and hazelnut flours are not only very forgiving but also make the cake inherently very moist. The addition of the spices used in the traditional *pain d'épices* gives it a certain *je ne sais quoi.* **YIELD: ONE 10-IN (25-CM) ROUND CAKE**

300 g/6 whole eggs

80 g/4 egg yolks

240 g/2$\frac{1}{2}$ cups hazelnut flour

120 g/1$\frac{1}{4}$ cups almond flour

30 g/3 tbsp cornstarch

2 g/$\frac{1}{2}$ tsp ground Ceylon cinnamon

2 g/$\frac{1}{2}$ tsp ground green cardamom

2 g/$\frac{1}{2}$ tsp ground cloves

250 g/1$\frac{1}{4}$ cups granulated sugar

12 g/1 tbsp vanilla bean paste (see Sources, page 216)

Grated zest of 1 orange (see page 110)

Grated zest of 1 lemon (see page 110)

Set the eggs out about 1 hour ahead of time to come to room temperature. Preheat the oven to 350°F (180°C). Line a rimmed baking sheet with parchment paper and spread the hazelnut and almond flours on the parchment. Toast in the oven for 5 to 6 minutes, or until they are a light golden brown and the aromas fill the room. Let cool to room temperature. Once cool, sift the nut flours with the cornstarch, cinnamon, cardamom, and cloves into a large bowl.

Coat the bottom and sides of a 10-in (25-cm) round cake pan with cooking spray, cut a piece of parchment paper to fit the bottom of the pan, and press it in to line the pan. Cut a second piece of parchment paper into a strip 2 in (5 cm) wide to line the inside edge of the pan and press it in to set.

Put the whole eggs, egg yolks, sugar, vanilla bean paste, orange zest, and lemon zest in a stand mixer fitted with a whisk attachment. Whip at high speed, until the mixture triples in size and forms stiff, pale peaks when pulled up with the whisk. (Be sure the eggs are at room temperature when you start; cold eggs at this stage will reach only half the volume needed.)

CONTINUED . . .

With the mixer on low speed, gently mix in the flour-cornstarch mixture, just until everything comes together. Take care not to deflate the batter. Gently pour the batter into the prepared cake pan.

Place into the center of the oven and bake for 10 minutes, or until a light golden brown crust forms on the top and the cake begins to visibly rise. Rotate the pan 180 degrees and bake for another 7 to 8 minutes, until the cake is golden brown and lightly bounces back to the touch. To check doneness, insert a paring knife straight into the center of the cake; it should come out clean and hot to the touch. Once the cake is done, remove it from the oven and set it on a cooling rack to cool to room temperature, 15 to 20 minutes. When the cake is cool to the touch, use an offset spatula to loosen the outside of the paper lining from the pan. Invert the cake over a plate or a baking sheet and then shake to release the cake from the pan. Remove the paper lining from the cake and reinvert it onto a plate or baking sheet so that the cake is right-side up.

The cake is best enjoyed immediately for the full nutty, spicy flavor. It can be prepared up to 3 days in advance and stored in an airtight container in a cool, dry place.

Sweet Note: Baking times vary greatly from oven to oven. Be sure not to open the oven door until you see that your cake has risen properly and has a very light golden layer set at the top. If you try to rotate the pan while the cake is still raw, it could deflate.

Given the complex flavor profile of this cake, it's delicious served simply with some whipped Mascarpone Chantilly (page 82), roasted peaches, or even chopped up on top of a bowl of silky Dark Chocolate Crémeux (page 161).

FRUIT & FLOWERS

It was a Saturday like most other Saturdays during August in San Francisco. I had arrived at the Ferry Plaza Farmers Market around seven in the morning to beat the rush of locals.

Early morning is when most of the local chefs come to the farmers' market, giving us time to reconnect with vendors and exchange stories. I was walking by the water with a steaming cup of coffee, considering what to purchase for the days ahead. Early morning at the Ferry Building, by the Embarcadero, as the fog lifts its curtain off the city and the bay, is always a Zen-inducing experience, and admittedly, I was moving slowly, enjoying the morning calm before another busy Saturday. Before I knew it, my senses were two steps ahead of me, and I was being drawn in.

I was intoxicated by a sweet scent as I walked by one of the many stands. The scent had the hint of honey and sweet blossoms. I had no choice but to gently lift a soft, perfectly ripe peach from the farmer's box. I was fixated on a small, white flower with a yellow center attached to the peach by a small branch. "Sex sells," said a jolly voice behind me.

It was my farmer friend Tory from Tory Farms in Dinuba, California. Standing tall, strong in stature, he reminds me of Jerry Garcia reincarnated with a purely jovial spirit. His glittering eyes always indicate that he is up to something sweet and mischievous. This is a man with secrets to share. I find that people who spend their time with their fingers deep in dirt, growing fruits and vegetables from seeds, have a secret that the rest of us just can't crack. The only thing genuinely sweeter and more delightful than Tory, his wife, Rebecca, and their children, are the fruits they grow and bring to market. They treat their produce like they treat their children, and as I treat my desserts: with love and care.

On this particular Saturday, Tory shared with me his real secret: sex. As much as we try to explain it, sell it, and capture it, Mother Nature has the real monopoly on sex and reproduction. We might think that as farmers, gardeners, and scientists, we have some control over it, but let's be real: Mother Nature doesn't need our help to create beautiful, sensuous, sweet, and sexy fruits and flowers. She does so in her own time. We have no true control in this game of eating natural things. And I very much love that. The true flavor and sensuousness of fruits and vegetables comes from eating seasonally and locally.

I believe that every season has its own emotions associated with it. Winter is full of solitude and introspection, and with spring comes blooming and exploration. Summer is a time of activity and fun, and autumn brings us back to earth with fiery colors and cooling temperatures. Mother Nature plays with these emotions in the fruits, flowers, and spices that she offers during the seasons. It's important

to remember this when planning your seasonal parties and purchasing fruits and flowers for the dessert you're creating.

Before my conversation with Tory about flowers and sex, and the naturally seductive powers of most fruit, I was drawn to nature's candy; I just hadn't put it into words. Today, I'm writing while my staff turn flats of tiny wild strawberries into a strawberry and vanilla bean preserve, and Tory's peaches into compote scented with organic lavender flowers. I feel so lucky to be in my kitchen at Tout Sweet during August, when I can grab the most luscious and sweet flavors of the most abundant season and preserve them for the rest of the year (or until we run out). The opening of this kitchen and pâtisserie has taught me many things, especially that everything comes at the right time. One of the most beautiful and astounding desserts is a perfectly ripe peach, grilled for one minute and served with a spoonful of chantilly and a drizzle of local honey. This dish takes all the patience and technique in the world—it takes knowing when the peaches are just right for such a simple presentation. If anyone in the Northern Hemisphere ever offers you this in early March, turn the other way. That peach is not ready for prime time.

Walking through the market in the summertime, I get overwhelmed. There are smells and tastes and sights that my eyes have not adjusted to yet. The summer season is so abundant with color and flavor, with sun-ripened everything. At just one stall, I recently counted five different varieties of peaches, and the farmer had limited himself because of the small space he has at the market. Here in California, I have access to different bushes, herbs, and flowers that have a strong aromatic flavor profile. What grows together naturally goes together, and matching flowers with the fruits they grow near creates a multilayered flavor profile: lemon verbena with peaches, rose geranium with berries and stone fruit. Try chamomile flowers, apricots, and nectarines in roasting or preserves. Fresh lavender blooms throughout the summer and is great with all summer fruit. Flower flavors have gotten a bad reputation. If your food tastes like a bar of soap, either there is too much of a good thing or imitation flavorings have been used. Fresh flowers from your farmer will bring a complex, astounding flavor profile that will enhance your dishes.

While I could go on and on about the summer season, let's not forget the pears and citrus fruits that become available in the cooler months. I tend to match these bits of winter sunshine with cloves, cinnamon, star anise, and cardamom. The woody spices are available in the cold months and will warm the palate and the heart. They can also stand up to roasting and braising, two common ways to prepare a warm dessert in the winter. I love to pull a jar of preserves from the freezer or canning shelf around the holidays, to add summer brightness to the earthy colors of winter.

The in-between seasons, spring and fall, also have a particular bounty and beauty. In the spring, we get to play with blooming flowers and new, fresh scents. I've included flowers in many of the recipes here, and you can continue to push yourself with flower waters and essences—just remember the rule: Fresh is fabulous. In the fall, we have fiery hues and earthy flavors. Pumpkins and butternut squash have beautiful color and match incredibly with sugars and spices. If you're looking to expand your repertoire, purchase a variety of squash at the farmers' market, take them home to roast in a 400°F (200°C) oven for 45 minutes, and taste away. Some of the most surprising and enjoyable desserts begin with easy taste experiments.

Mother Nature may play a game with my emotions as the seasons come and go, but I can't thank her enough. She is a kind mistress to follow. I wish I were brilliant enough to translate emotions into fruits; instead, I get to take my inspiration from Mother Nature and get most of the credit. It should come as no surprise that I encourage you to play with your food, and now I encourage you to play with your emotions and those of your guests. The surprises that come when we delve into nature's bounty are truly delightful.

choosing fruit

Fruit may be nature's candy, but take a bite of anything out of season and it may put you off of that fruit for a long time. I have had an especially blessed life when it comes to fruit. I was lucky enough to be born in Turkey, a country with a perfect climate and ancient cultivation techniques for figs, apricots, and apples, not to mention sour cherries, which I adore. Perhaps a part of my love of dessert creation is a constant search for the flavor profiles of my childhood. Food memories are powerful things. In my adult life, I've lived in different parts of the United States, but most of my time has been spent in California. We not only have happy cows, we also have happy, thriving fruit trees. I count my lucky stars every Saturday morning that I walk the farmers' market or just wander into a well-stocked produce aisle. We can order flats of ripe nectarines and tomatoes from our local farmers on Thursday, and I can drive 5 minutes to pick them up from a local farmers' market on Saturday, knowing they were hand-picked off the trees the day before. That is a miracle of modern systems, and I don't take it for granted.

When you're shopping for fruit, pay attention to what you're getting. Using the best ingredients will completely change your dessert and make the time, love, and effort all worth it. More than we do with any other food, we have control over the quality of fruit that we use, so take your time and use these tips:

1. Talk to your farmer or grocer. Ask what's best, ask what to look for, ask what came in or was picked this morning. The calendar may say that apples are in season, but different varieties will have the best flavor, depending on factors such as whether it has been a dry year or a cold, rainy one.

2. Follow your nose. Fruit should smell clean and bright and give off the sweet smells that you would expect of that particular fruit. A ripe, well-cultivated, in-season strawberry will smell like a strawberry. An unripe, poorly raised, out-of-season strawberry will smell like wax or may not give off any smell at all. If you smell any hint of mold or a bitter, sour smell, the fruit is probably past its prime and should be discarded.

3. Use your eyes. Choose fruit that is the color it should be and check for mold. This is also an area where farmers can teach us a lot. My farmer friend Tory once pointed out the rough, pulled-together skin on a pluot (a plum-apricot hybrid). I thought they were blemishes. He taught me that they are an indication that the fruit has had good access to sunshine during its life and that the sugars are gathering just under the skin. It was one of the sweetest, most sultry and well-textured pluots—for that matter, the sweetest, most sultry apricot or plum—I've ever eaten. Farmers are my secret weapon in choosing fruit. Meet the farmers or produce grocers in your town and find your own secret weapon.

4. Be intrigued and be adventurous. There are so many varieties of fruit available to us, and many of them are better at different times of the year. Remember, farmers have mortgages and utility bills to pay all year long just like the rest of us do. It benefits them to cultivate fruit, every season, that is tasty. If you have a favorite variety of apple, you may notice that at certain times of the year it isn't as tasty as at others. Variety is the spice of life, and this is particularly true in the fruit world. Besides farmers' markets, Asian, Mexican, and other ethnic markets tend to carry fruits and vegetables that aren't available in other places. I have a recipe for Buddha's hand in this book. This is a fruit that I didn't know existed until I was twenty years old. Explore the produce aisles, ask questions, and try out new fruit.

• • •

citrus zest

Oranges, limes, grapefruit, and lemons are only the beginning of the citrus family. Talk about nature's candy! Each is an edible, vitamin-packed bit of wonderful. The acid in citrus brings balance to many dishes, sweet and savory. Each variety of citrus fruit has its own flavor profile, and most of them open the palate to tasting dormant elements of other ingredients. Besides the juice inside the fruit, the very outside of a citrus fruit has its own treasure trove of secrets. Peel an orange and then bend the peel against the natural curve of the fruit. A spray of essential oils will come out, showering everything in its way with a shiny, shimmering coating. There is a certain ineffable—some might say umami—flavor and scent to citrus essential oils. Why discard them? Use them! A quick word of caution: Zest that still has the pith, or white part, attached to it can ruin a dish. When zesting, be vigilant: Always rinse (you don't know how many people have handled that fruit), use only the outermost layer of the peel, and use firm, glossy fruit.

In the following pages, there are several recipes that call for the zest of an orange or a lemon. I love zest. I mean, say it with me: "Zest!" Even the word is amazing. Zest is zesty! It brings out flavor, adds to the complexity of the taste profile, and is a simple, beautiful garnish. Using the zest of a fruit rounds out the flavors of a baked or cooked dessert and adds to the complexity of a fruit juice or fresh cocktail.

There are two ways that I call for citrus zest in my recipes:

GRATED ZEST: When I call for "Grated zest of 1 orange," I'm asking you to use a Microplane, zester, or other small, hand-held grater to pull off the most outside layer of the entire fruit. To do this quickly with a Microplane, hold the Microplane in your dominant hand with the grater-side down. Use your thumb to guide the Microplane along the surface of the fruit, turning as you go. This will ensure that you get all the zest and none of the pith, and the upturned grater will catch the zest curls as you work.

STRIPS OF ZEST: In other recipes, I call for a "2-in (5-cm) strip of zest." Here, I'm looking for an intact piece of zest that will most likely be discarded after giving up its essential oils and flavor. You can cut off a strip of zest with a zester, a vegetable peeler, or a sharp knife. The key here is to keep the zest intact so that it can be removed and discarded easily.

put the fruit to work

What's not to love about a jar of naturally sweet, tangy fruit preserved at the height of ripeness and opened in the gray, leafless days of winter? It is still one of the joys of my life to know that a day of cleaning, cooking, and canning fruit will lead to many fruit-filled days to come. And you don't have to wait for the winter chill to enjoy a good fruit purée or sauce. A fruit picked, cooked, and eaten on the same day or in the same week is an amazing treat. The most amazing thing about it is that fruit comes with some of its own preservatives, its own flavors, and its own thickener. We add sugar, other fruits or flavorings, and pectin to enhance these qualities. But isn't it incredible that all those things come from nature? It blows my mind that all this is just a simple addition to pump up and speed up what is already naturally there.

I love to have fruit purées and sauces available in my freezer year-round. They don't take long to thaw, and they add an entirely new dimension to desserts. At the end of summer, I can be found scoring flats of overripe fruits at a low cost and then sneaking them back to my kitchen to purée and freeze. The high cost of organic fruits means that one should get the most out of their bounty, especially when it is at its most spectacular. Mixing a berry purée into a meringue or drizzling a reduced berry sauce over shortcakes adds a tangy, sweet, rounded flavor to the entire dish.

Fruit, like many natural food products, breaks down with time and heat. Sugar also helps to break down some of fruit's natural barriers by drawing water out and adding to the juicy goodness of a purée or jam, and in addition it preserves the texture and flavor of the fruit. Adding a squeeze of lemon juice to a purée or jam keeps the final product loyal to the original color of the fruit. You may have noticed that after freezing, certain fruit, especially apples and bananas, becomes brown, oxidized, and unappealing, no matter how much air you squeeze out of the resealable bag or how much you mummify them with plastic wrap. A little bit of lemon goes a long way in preventing the natural oxidization and preserving the beautiful color. Keep in mind that oxidized fruit is not bad fruit. You can still make a hearty banana bread or bake the apples into a cake. Tossing good fruit is fruit abuse—there's always a way to put it to use. A simple purée will also work: Clean and blend the fruit, along with granulated sugar amounting to 10 percent of the weight of the fruit and a touch of lemon juice. Freeze this magical mixture in an airtight container for up to 6 months; to avoid freezer burn, cover the container with two layers of plastic wrap and then seal it with the lid. This will reduce the amount of air that gets into the container.

Once you get comfortable playing with purée and jam ratios, you can begin to play with the flavors and fruit combinations, as well as the amounts of sugar and lemon. A basic ratio for a jam is to add sugar amounting to 80 percent of the weight of the fruit. For example, for $1/2$ kg/1 lb of berries, you would use approximately 400 g/2 cups of sugar. Most jams include a bit of lemon juice; for this recipe you would use 12 g/1 tbsp.

Each fruit has different amounts of water, sugar, and pectin, and they also vary depending on the time of year that the fruit is picked. Take strawberries as an example. In March, when they first appear at the farmers' market, they have begun to plump up and turn red, with a lot of water and a bit of sugar. As we move into early summer, the strawberries at the market are smaller and sweeter. Finally, in August, strawberries are at their smallest size but have a high sugar and pectin ratio to their weight. Strawberries at every time are delicious and have something wonderful to offer. Knowing your produce and its makeup means that you can use it to its highest potential.

Just as making a sorbet involves more than merely adding simple syrup to any fruit purée, not all fruit will behave the same in the previous ratio for making jams. Each fruit has a different water-sugar-pectin ratio. When creating jams and marmalades, you will sometimes need to introduce additional pectin into the recipe, depending on the fruit and the desired final consistency. Pectin is a natural gelling agent that occurs in most fruit, but only to a certain extent. Most professional kitchens use store-bought powdered pectins, which are easy to scale and work with in a consistent manner. However, I've also made my own pectin by cooking the pits and peels of particular fruits, which breaks down the natural pectin. Explore this further in your own kitchen. High-fiber, high-pectin fruits include apples, citrus peel, pears, and cranberries. Extracting pectin is done through a simple process of cooking the peels, cores, and pith in a pectin bag (even a clean, thin white pillowcase will do) and then squeezing the pectin out of the cooked fruit to obtain liquid pectin. This is a simple, fun, and natural way to extract pectin, and it excites the food science geek inside of me. But powdered pectin is something that you can readily have on hand, and it is also consistent in its potency and easy to mix into preparations. Always cook your pectin into the jam so that its gelling power is fully activated and the jam will set as it cools.

A fruit coulis is a simple combination of sugar and fruit, blended and strained to create a smooth, glossy final product to be poured over ice cream or cake, or as an addition to a well-whipped chantilly. If you want a more refined preparation for a coulis, cook it with a small amount of pectin, bringing it to a quick boil, and then chill it in the refrigerator. The pectin will bind the water molecules, creating a more supple texture that won't "bleed" once on the plate.

A compote is a stewed fruit dessert that is usually served with bits of the fruit swimming in a fruit syrup. Compote is a great way to use fruit in the winter that was either frozen or dried earlier in the year. It generally begins with simple syrup, to which the chopped fruit is added, to be stewed down over low heat. A compote can be made up of one fruit or several that complement one another. Add some citrus zest and a squeeze of lemon to both preserve the color and bump up the flavor of the dish. If you're looking for a more adult approach to fruit, add cut ripe stone fruit to bourbon and let it sit for 2 days. Strain and serve—I promise you'll have a crowd pleaser.

CITRUS SUPRÊMES

Suprêmes are a simple yet beautiful cut of citrus fruit, and I encourage you to master them. A citrus suprême is achieved by cutting off the peel and pith (the white part that usually stays on when the fruit is peeled by hand) and then cutting out the sections of the fruit. This removes the bitter membrane and leaves only half-moons of juicy, glossy fruit. The key to this technique is a sharp paring knife and a steady hand. Citrus fruits give us a rainbow of colors and sweet, tongue-awakening, acidic juice throughout the year. They have a starring role in many desserts because they stand up to baking, cut through creams and chocolates, and bring their own unique flavor to a dish without being overpowering. The suprême cut gives us the chance to see their beauty on the plate as well as taste it.

1. Cut the bottom $1/8$ in (4 mm) off the fruit to create a flat surface.

2. Use a small, sharp knife to cut between the peel and the fruit, following the natural curve of the fruit and moving in one curving motion from the top all the way to the cutting board. You should have a citrus disco ball—a shiny, peel- and pith-free fruit with the sections extremely evident.

3. Use a sharp paring knife to cut along the membrane of each section. Slide the knife into the fruit along the membrane on either side of each suprême and then pop the half-moon-shaped section out with the knife.

These can be a beautiful, shiny garnish for cakes or the central fruit on a tart. The suprême is just that—the supreme, most luscious part of the fruit.

simple fruit sauce

This is a crash course in preparing a sweet, simple, and beautiful sauce with a few basic ingredients. Whether you are macerating a beautiful bowl of fruit or using it to add flavor and flair to your presentation, this simple knowledge is good to have in your back pocket. Adding pectin to a fruit purée produces a beautiful, homogeneous sauce that holds up well on the plate and has a wonderful, velvety texture.

1. Place the fruit purée in a saucepan. Over low heat, warm it to 122°F (50°C); hot to the touch.

2. In a separate mixing bowl, use a whisk to evenly combine the sugar and pectin.

3. Slowly sprinkle the sugar mixture into the saucepan, stirring to combine.

4. Cook over high heat, whisking continuously, until it comes to a boil.

5. Keep whisking and allow the mixture to boil for 30 seconds.

6. Transfer to a clean bowl and set the bowl into an ice bath. Allow the mixture to cool.

7. Store in an airtight container in the refrigerator for up to 2 weeks.

---

basic berry sauce

YIELD: ³/₄ CUP (180 ML)

250 g/³/₄ cup raspberry or blackberry purée

5 g/1 tsp lemon juice

30 g/2 tbsp plus 1¹/₂ tsp granulated sugar

3 g/¹/₂ tsp apple pectin powder

Add the lemon juice to the puréed fruit and proceed as directed. This is a great sauce to work from as you get more creative with fruit combinations.

---

passion fruit, mango & lime sauce

Passion fruit is very low in pectin, but mango has quite a bit. Make sure to use a very ripe mango, as the fibers in an underripe fruit will change the flavors and textures of the sauce. Mango purée and passion fruit purée are commonly available in many specialty grocery stores. I have a not-so-secret love affair with passion fruit. I've often said that if I were to be reincarnated, I'd like to come back as a passion fruit. **YIELD: 1 CUP (240 ML)**

200 g/²/₃ cup passion fruit purée

100 g/¹/₃ cup mango purée

15 g/1 tbsp lime juice, plus grated zest of 1 lime (see page 110)

5 g/1 tsp apple pectin powder

In this recipe, I add the lime juice to the puréed fruit and the zest after the sauce is cooked and cooled, to avoid oxidation. Cooking also destroys a lot of the essential oils of the zest. Adding it once the sauce is cool will preserve the color and essence of the flavor.

---

raspberry & red verjus sauce

Verjus is a delicious cross between wine and vinegar; it's not as sweet as wine and not as pungent as vinegar. I like to use it with berries, particularly red berries, because it complements their sweet and tart flavor profile. **YIELD: 1 CUP (240 ML)**

175 g/¹/₂ cup raspberry purée

75 g/¹/₄ cup Bing cherry purée

35 g/3 tbsp granulated sugar

5 g/1 tsp apple pectin powder

25 g/1¹/₂ tbsp red verjus (see Sources, page 216)

Add the red verjus after the purée and sugar mixture comes to a boil, in the last 30 seconds of the cooking process. This way the vinegar will not cook out and the verjus will retain its bold, crisp flavor.

warm strawberry— pinot noir sauce

I was introduced to this wonderful sauce when I worked at the Meeting House in San Francisco. I recall our pastry chef, Noah, pouring entire bottles of Pinot Noir over strawberries that were sprinkled with sugar and vanilla. As a young pastry cook, I thought, "If this is what a pastry chef is, sign me up!" The first time I made this sauce in the Meeting House kitchen, I strained it, tasted it, and couldn't stop drinking it. The owner, Joanna, told me, "It's not sangria; put it back on the flame." Needless to say, the sauce is delicious before the alcohol is cooked off, but it's decadent when reduced to a sweeter, mature berry-wine sauce. It begs to be soaked up into something delicious. Shortcakes, anyone? **YIELD: 2 CUPS (480 ML)**

---

1 kg/4 cups very ripe or thawed frozen sweet strawberries

1 vanilla bean or 12 g/1 tbsp vanilla bean paste (see Sources, page 216)

250 g/1¼ cups granulated sugar

One 2-in (5-cm) strip orange zest (see page 110)

5 g/2 tsp whole black peppercorns

750 g/one 750-ml bottle Pinot Noir

Prepare the strawberries by rinsing and cutting off the green hulls. Split the vanilla bean in half lengthwise with a paring knife and then use the knife to scrape the seeds from the pod. Reserve both the seeds and the pod.

In a large, clean mixing bowl, combine the sugar with the prepared vanilla seeds and pod or vanilla bean paste, orange zest, and black peppercorns. Use clean fingers to rub the aromatics into the sugar and fully combine the mixture. This will release the fragrant essential oils into the sugar.

Toss the sugar mixture with the strawberries to coat. Pour the entire bottle of Pinot Noir over the strawberry-sugar mixture and stir to mix everything together. Cover the top of the bowl with plastic wrap; double-wrap it to ensure that the seal will stay tight during cooking.

Bring a saucepan of water to a low simmer. Place the covered bowl over the simmering water to create a bain-marie. Be sure that the water is not touching the bowl. Cook the fruit mixture over the water on medium heat for 1 to 1½ hours, or until the berries start to break down and steam pushes up on the plastic wrap.

Occasionally check the water in the pan, making sure it doesn't boil away. Remove the bowl from the heat. Keep the bowl covered and let it sit at room temperature until cool, about 1 hour. When cool, place the bowl in the refrigerator to chill for at least 4 hours, or overnight.

When the mixture is chilled and you are ready to work, remove the plastic wrap. Line a large, fine-mesh strainer with cheesecloth. Set the strainer over a clean, large bowl so that there is a good amount of space between the strainer and the bowl. Put the bowl with the strainer into the sink. Pour the berry mixture into the cheesecloth-lined strainer, and let it sit for 30 minutes to 1 hour. Let gravity do its work so that all the juices flow into the bowl. Do not press or push; you don't want to force extra seeds or bits of the berries into the bowl.

When all the liquid has strained into the bowl, discard the fruit left in the cheesecloth.

Pour the berry mixture into a medium stainless-steel or enamel-coated saucepan and bring to a simmer over low heat. Cook the mixture, uncovered, for 5 to 10 minutes to allow the liquid to reduce. When done, the mixture will have thickened and will fall slowly off a spoon, like syrup.

The sauce is ready to be used immediately. It can be kept in an airtight container in the refrigerator for up to 1 week. Always warm this sauce gently before using.

spring berries & bing cherries macerated in raspberry & red verjus sauce

By the time strawberries and raspberries start to appear at the market, spring and summer are upon us. This means bright flavors and colors. Here, I combine them with Bing cherries, which take the flavor to a whole new level. Make this dish at a time when both fresh berries and cherries are available in your market. Macerating fruit is the easiest way to elevate an already wonderfully delicious taste. Whenever I serve macerated berries as a part of a dessert, people go crazy for them. Who can resist the temptation of a luscious berry? **YIELD: 3 CUPS (710 ML)**

---

250 g/1 cup **Bing cherries**

250 g/1 cup **small organic strawberries**

340 g/2 cups **red raspberries**

50 g/¼ cup **Raspberry & Red Verjus Sauce (page 115)**

Prepare the fruit by pitting and halving the cherries; hull the strawberries and cut them in half; keep the raspberries whole.

In a clean, medium bowl, combine all of the fruit; cover with the sauce and use a rubber spatula to gently fold until the fruit is coated in sauce. Let sit for 30 minutes to allow the flavors to marry together. Enjoy immediately.

Sweet Note: Keep in mind that macerating the berries more than 1 hour in advance will cause the sugars and acid to break down the fruits, and the water will begin to seep out. This may look messier on the plate, but it will still be quite tasty.

basic berry jam

Mornings are sacred to me. The first sensations of the morning determine my state of mind for the rest of the day. The simplicity of a really delicious jam with some salted butter and great toast can be surpassed only by the addition of a great coffee! I think this is why everyone's pantry deserves to have some great jam. At Tout Sweet, I'm always pushing to create delicious, balanced, and creative jams. Our Black Velvet (pluot, apricot, sour cherry) may be my favorite. It's just sexy! Here, I wanted to introduce the most basic method of jam making, and bring it back to childhood—a great raspberry jam. After you master this bad boy, feel free to put on your creative hat and explore your own combinations. **YIELD: 4 CUPS (960 ML)**

---

450 g/3²/₃ cups ripe raspberries or any ripe berry

50 g/3 tbsp fresh, strained orange juice

30 g/2 tbsp lemon juice

200 g/1 cup granulated sugar

5 g/1 tsp apple pectin powder

Prepare the berries by gently rinsing them in a colander under cool running water. Discard the water. In a 4-qt (3.8-L) stainless-steel or enamel-coated saucepan, combine the berries, orange juice, and lemon juice; stir to coat the berries.

In a small bowl, whisk together the sugar and pectin.

Cover the berry mixture with the pectin and sugar. Use a rubber spatula to press down on the fruit; this will break down the berries and incorporate the sugar-pectin. Over medium heat, cook the mixture for 3 to 5 minutes, or until the berries break down and release their juices. Stir the mixture occasionally with a spatula to combine the mixture and to ensure that the berries and sugar do not stick to the bottom.

When the berries begin to release their juices, turn up the heat so that the mixture comes to a boil. Allow it to boil for 4 to 6 minutes, stirring occasionally and scraping the bottom so that the

jam doesn't burn. This will break down the berries, and the heat will cause the pectin to react.

Pour the hot berry jam into a glass bowl and let it cool to room temperature. Cover the jam with plastic wrap by placing the wrap directly onto the surface of the jam so that a skin does not form, and let it sit at room temperature for 1 hour, or until the jam shines and has a thick, jelly consistency. Store in an airtight container in the refrigerator for up to 5 days.

This jam can be canned when it is hot to preserve it for up to 1 year.

Sweet Note: For a seedless jam, purée the berries in a blender or food processor and then strain out the seeds through a fine-mesh sieve. Combine the ingredients, blend everything again until you have a smooth purée, and then strain again through a fine-mesh sieve. Transfer to a stainless-steel or enamel-coated saucepan and cook as directed.

chilled summer berry soup with lillet rosé

I first saw chilled fruit "consommé," or clear soup, in New York. At the time I recall thinking, "Wow, this is elegant!" And it's a great way to use overripe berries. In fact, when I want to make a big batch of this soup, I go to the farmers' market and ask them for overripe and bruised berries. Farmers are happy to unload them at a discounted price, and I always walk away with a smirk on my face. I add a little bit of Lillet Rosé—why not? Sweet summer berries are so flirtatious on their own, and the Lillet gives the soup another hint of feminine elegance. **YIELD: 1^1/$_2$ CUPS (360 ML)**

---

1 vanilla bean or 12 g/1 tbsp vanilla bean paste (see Sources, page 216)

1 kg/4 cups very ripe or thawed frozen strawberries, raspberries, blueberries, or blackberries

150 g/^{3}/$_4$ cup granulated sugar

75 g/^{1}/$_3$ cup Lillet Rosé aperitif

Split the vanilla bean in half lengthwise with a paring knife and then use the knife to scrape the seeds from the pod. Place the berries, sugar, vanilla seeds and pod or vanilla bean paste into a medium glass or stainless-steel mixing bowl. Cover the bowl with plastic wrap; double-wrap it to ensure that the seal will stay tight during cooking.

Bring a saucepan of water to a low simmer. Place the covered bowl over the simmering water to create a bain-marie. Be sure that the water is not touching the bowl. Cook the fruit mixture for 1 to 1^1/$_2$ hours, or until the berries start to break down and steam pushes up on the plastic wrap. Occasionally check the water in the pan, making sure it doesn't boil away. Remove the bowl from the heat. Keep the bowl covered and leave it at room temperature until cool, about 1 hour. When cool,

place the bowl in the refrigerator to chill for at least 4 hours or up to 1 day.

After 4 hours, remove the plastic wrap. Line a large fine-mesh strainer with cheesecloth. Set the strainer over a clean, large bowl so that there is a good amount of space between the strainer and the bowl. Put the bowl with the strainer into the sink. Pour the berry mixture into the cheesecloth-lined strainer and let it sit for 30 minutes to 1 hour. Let gravity do its work so that all of the juices flow into the bowl. Do not press or push; you don't want to force extra seeds or bits of the berries into the bowl. When the juices have drained, discard the fruit left in the cheesecloth. Transfer to an airtight container and chill in the refrigerator for up to 1 week. When ready to serve the soup, mix in the Lillet Rosé to accentuate the floral flavor.

blackberry & lemon verbena soda

When I can, I try to create sodas as a dessert. Sweet and complex blackberries play beautifully with the vibrant aromas of fresh lemon verbena. And a touch of crème de mûre gives the soda a subtle but robust and round flavor. **YIELD: 4 CUPS (960 ML)**

---

1 kg/4 cups ripe blackberries

One 2-in (5-cm) strip of lemon zest (see page 110)

4 fresh lemon verbena leaves

225 g/1 cup plus 2 tbsp granulated sugar

3 tbsp crème de mûre

1 L artisanal soda water

Rinse the blackberries under cool running water. Set them aside in a colander to drain completely.

In a large heat-resistant bowl, combine the lemon zest, lemon verbena leaves, and sugar. Use clean fingers to rub the aromatics and sugar together. Add the blackberries and gently toss to coat the berries with sugar. Cover the bowl with plastic wrap; double-wrap it to ensure that the seal will stay tight during cooking.

Bring a saucepan of water to a low simmer. Place the covered bowl over the simmering water to create a bain-marie. Be sure that the water does not touch the bowl. Cook the mixture for 1 to 1½ hours, or until the berries start to break down and steam pushes up on the plastic wrap. Occasionally check the water in the pan, making sure it doesn't boil away. Remove the bowl from the heat. Keep the bowl covered and leave it at room temperature until cool. When cooled, place it in the refrigerator for at least 4 hours, or overnight.

When you are ready to work, remove the plastic wrap. Pour the berry mixture into a cheesecloth-lined strainer set into a large bowl and let it sit for 30 minutes to 1 hour. Let all the juices flow into the bowl. Do not press or push; you don't want to force extra seeds or bits of the berries into the bowl. When all the liquid has strained through, remove the strainer from the bowl and discard the fruit.

Add the crème de mûre to the blackberry syrup and stir with a wooden spoon. In a 10-oz (300-ml) glass, pour 6 oz (180 ml) of the soda water. Add 2 oz (60 ml) of the blackberry syrup to the top of the glass and serve. The beautiful, velvety syrup will sit on top of the soda until you or your guest mixes it in.

blood orange, grapefruit & campari gelée

Sometimes people ask me, "Is *gelée* just a fancy word for Jell-O?" To which I reply, "If by *Jell-O* you mean an awesome, delicious, sophisticated dessert that surprises and delights, then yes." With this recipe, you be the judge. When I was on *Top Chef: Just Desserts*, we had a challenge to create a dessert based on our favorite cocktail. This gelée came from my love of the classic Negroni and features citrus notes and flavor with a kick of Campari. If you can't get blood oranges, use all grapefruit juice. **YIELD: 4 SERVINGS**

---

9 g/1 tbsp powdered gelatin or 3 silver gelatin leaves

100 g/1½ cups granulated sugar

90 g/¼ cup plus 2 tbsp water

90 g/¼ cup plus 2 tbsp fresh grapefruit juice

140 g/½ cup fresh blood orange juice

70 g/1¼ cup plus 1 tbsp Campari

If using powdered gelatin, sprinkle it over a small bowl of cool water, or bloom the gelatin leaves by placing them in a bowl of ice water for 5 minutes. Remove the leaves of gelatin from the water and squeeze out the water.

While the gelatin is blooming, combine the sugar and 90 g/¼ cup plus 2 tbsp water in a small stainless-steel or enamel-coated saucepan and heat to boiling. Remove from the heat. Add the gelatin directly to the boiling simple syrup.

In a separate small bowl, combine the citrus juices, then add to the saucepan with the syrup and gelatin and whisk to incorporate. Add the

Campari and whisk to combine. Remove the saucepan from the heat. You will have a translucent, orange-pink, shimmering liquid.

Place an egg carton upside-down on a baking sheet. Divide the gelée among four stemless wineglasses, pouring about 3 oz (90 ml) into each glass. Set the glasses at a 45-degree angle on the egg carton and gently transfer the entire baking sheet to the refrigerator. Allow to cool for 2 to 3 hours, or until the gelée sets completely.

strawberry-lime sorbet

Have you ever experienced New York City in August? It is hot and sticky, and the search for a cool, sweet treat begins early in the day. When I lived in New York, my friends laughed at my obsession with Mr. Softy, a traveling truck with soft-serve ice cream that I would happily stand in line for. While we don't get the same sticky, wet summer heat in San Francisco, I will still take a soft-serve ice cream cone with sprinkles any day. This refreshing sorbet, with its kick of acidity, was my response to soft-serve ice cream—a little bit of refreshment on a hot day. **YIELD: 3 CUPS (720 ML)**

---

670 g/3 cups strawberry purée

20 g/1 tbsp corn syrup or glucose syrup (see Sources, page 216)

15 g/2 tsp lime syrup

15 g/1 tbsp lime juice

Grated zest of 1 lime (see page 110)

Place the strawberry purée into a large glass or stainless-steel bowl and set aside.

In a medium stainless-steel or enamel-coated saucepan, combine the corn syrup and lime syrup and place over medium heat. Stir gently until the mixture comes together. Remove from the heat and pour into the bowl of strawberry purée. Use a whisk to combine until evenly mixed. Cover the bowl with plastic wrap and set in the refrigerator for 2 hours, or overnight, to chill completely.

In a small bowl, mix the lime juice and lime zest together. Remove the strawberry-syrup mixture from the refrigerator and stir in the lime mixture.

Freeze in an ice-cream maker according to the manufacturer's specifications. Serve cold. Store in an airtight container in the freezer up to 2 weeks.

meyer lemon curd

All curds are not created equal. The key to a good lemon curd is fresh lemon juice. Bottled lemon juice has been pasteurized, which adds a metallic astringency that comes through strongly in a preparation like curd. The curd also needs to have a balance of acidity, sugar, and creamy fatty goodness. Be sure to cook the custard properly, and add the butter at the right time and the right temperature. We are performing alchemy, after all. **YIELD: 4 CUPS (960 ML)**

---

170 g/³/₄ cup unsalted butter

280 g/1 cup plus 3 tbsp fresh Meyer lemon juice

Grated zest of 1 Meyer lemon (see page 110)

180 g/1 cup granulated sugar

200 g/4 whole eggs

160 g/8 egg yolks

Use a sharp knife to cut the butter into 1-in (2.5-cm) cubes. Place the butter in a bowl on the countertop for 30 minutes to bring to room temperature. Meanwhile, set up a medium bowl with a fine-mesh strainer. Fill a separate, larger bowl with ice.

Pour the lemon juice into a stainless-steel or enamel-coated 4-qt (3.8-L) saucepan and add the lemon zest. Place the saucepan over medium heat. In a separate medium bowl, whisk together the sugar, whole eggs, and egg yolks. Temper the egg mixture by adding ¹/₄ cup (60 ml) of the warm lemon juice to the egg mixture, while stirring. Continue to add warm lemon juice to the egg mixture until the mixture in the bowl is warm. This will keep the eggs from scrambling. Add the tempered egg mixture back to the saucepan and cook, stirring constantly with a rubber spatula, until the mixture is 180°F (82°C). Immediately pour the mixture into the fine-mesh strainer and strain it into the bowl. Put the bowl of strained custard into the prepared ice bath. Cool in the ice bath until it is 95° to 104°F (35° to 40°C).

Remove the bowl of custard from the ice bath and add the butter. Use a handheld mixer to emulsify the custard and butter.

The curd can be used immediately as a filling for a tart, or you can store it in an airtight container in the refrigerator for up to 2 weeks.

Sweet Note: If you really want to blow your own mind, replace the Meyer lemon juice with passion fruit juice and reduce the sugar by 20 g (1¹/₂ tbsp).

candied buddha's hand

The fruit known as Buddha's hand is such a beautiful wonder. I love seeing their irregular and curious variations at the market. I'm likely to be found scratching their skin to smell their sweet and fragrant perfume. However, I really couldn't think of many ways to use them, as they have very little fruit and no juice. One day my former sous chef Carol, who is a brilliantly talented library of pastry information, came in with candied cross sections of Buddha's hands. I have been doing this, with delight and gratitude, every winter since. When candied, the Buddha's hand has a very delicate and subtle flavor. I love using these as a part of a plated dessert, and I sometimes let them dry overnight on a cooling rack set over a baking pan, and toss them in sugar to crystallize, so that I can decorate tarts and cakes with them. And don't you dare throw the syrup away. A little splash into an evening cocktail will put a smile on anyone's face. **YIELD: 3 CUPS (645 G)**

1 large Buddha's hand

2 kg/8 cups water

700 g/3$^1/_2$ cups granulated sugar

100 g/$^1/_3$ cup corn syrup
or glucose syrup (see Sources, page 216)

45 g/3 tbsp lemon juice

Preheat the oven to 300°F (150°C). Rinse the Buddha's hand under cool running water. Cut the "fingers" off the fruit so that there is a nice, round stalk left. (Reserve the fingers for another use, such as making infusions and compotes.) Use an electric or Japanese mandoline or a very sharp knife to slice the stalk into very thin slices; set aside.

Combine the water, sugar, and corn syrup in a large saucepan. Bring to a boil over high heat and boil for about 5 minutes, until completely combined, to make a syrup. The syrup should still be clear and thin. Turn off the heat and add the lemon juice. Transfer the syrup to a 9-by-13-by-2-in (23-by-33-by-5-cm) baking pan or glass baking dish. Immediately lay all the slices

flat in the syrup; use tongs, as the syrup will still be hot. Cover the pan with aluminum foil and place it in the oven. Allow the Buddha's hand slices to poach in the syrup for 1$^1/_2$ to 2 hours, until the slices are translucent. When you pick up one of the slices, it should be floppy but still keep its shape.

Remove the foil from the baking pan. Return it to the oven and continue to bake for 20 minutes, or until the syrup has a velvety, maple-syrup consistency. Remove the pan from the oven and allow the fruit and syrup to cool at room temperature for 1 hour. Transfer the Buddha's hand slices and syrup to an airtight container and refrigerate for up to 1 month.

bing cherries braised in syrah & star anise

These wine-glazed cherries are so delicious you'll be spooning them straight into your mouth from the pan. Ripe summer Bing cherries are juicy and sweet, and star anise has a natural deep licorice flavor that adds spice and balance to the sweetness of summer fruit like cherries. Since most good Syrah wines are described as having cherry and anise notes, it is no wonder these three flavors marry well. **YIELD: 4 CUPS (1.5 KG)**

---

1 kg/4 cups fresh Bing cherries

½ vanilla bean or 6 g/1½ tsp vanilla bean paste (see Sources, page 216)

200 g/1 cup granulated sugar

3 star anise pods

750 g/one 750-ml bottle medium-quality Syrah

50 g/2 tbsp plus 1½ tsp smooth sour cherry jam (found at most European markets)

Use fresh Bing cherries that are firm and ripe. If they are bruised or overripe, be sure to keep your eye on them while cooking to prevent overcooking. Pit the cherries, halve them, and reserve in a bowl.

Split the vanilla bean in half lengthwise with a paring knife, and then use the knife to scrape the seeds from the pod. Reserve both the seeds and the pod.

In a medium bowl, mix the sugar with the vanilla seeds and pod or vanilla bean paste and star anise pods. Use clean fingers to rub the aromatics into the sugar and fully combine the mixture. This will release the fragrant essential oils into the sugar.

Pour the Syrah into a straight-sided stainless-steel or enamel-coated saucepan, 10 in (25 cm) in diameter. Add the sugar mixture and cook over medium heat until reduced by one-third.

Stir occasionally, scraping the bottom so that the sugar does not burn. Using a fork or heat-resistant tongs, remove the vanilla pod and star anise. Add the sour cherry jam; whisk together to emulsify the mixture of wine, sugar, and cherry jam. Remove from the heat.

Gently place the cherries into the wine reduction. Toss lightly to coat. Cook over medium heat for 2 to 3 minutes, or until the cherries just start to break down but are still firm. I like to let the cherries sit in their juices at room temperature for 5 to 10 minutes, absorbing and soaking in all the flavor. When ready to serve, warm them up gently over low heat.

Sweet Note: Five words: Tahitian Vanilla Bean Ice Cream (page 92). Put the tiniest pinch of Maldon flake sea salt on top to awaken your palate.

lemongrass poached rhubarb

Poaching allows rhubarb to keep some of its integrity, something that I think we should allow all our food to do. If you use larger pieces of rhubab for dramatic effect, as pictured here, make sure you poach it longer. The colors of this dish are pink, green, and sexy, and the fragrant aromas of lemongrass and orange zest bring a balance and depth to it. This is wonderful served cold in the summer months. **YIELD: 4 CUPS (2 KG)**

---

910 g/2 lb fresh rhubarb, preferably thin stalks

2 fresh lemongrass stalks

15 g/about a 2-in (5-cm) piece fresh ginger

2 kg/8^1/$_2$ cups water

650 g/3^1/$_4$ cups granulated sugar

Three 2-in (5-cm) strips orange zest (see page 110)

75 g/^{1}/$_4$ cup grenadine syrup

Tahitian Vanilla Bean Ice Cream (page 92) or Strawberry-Lime Sorbet (page 126) for serving

---

Rinse the rhubarb under cool water and cut it into ^{1}/$_4$-in (6-mm) slices. If very thick, use a paring knife to cut the stalks in half lengthwise to about ^{1}/$_2$ in (1 cm) thick. Place the rhubarb pieces into a medium bowl and set aside. Cut the lemongrass into 1-in (2.5-cm) slices. Lay the flat side of a knife on the slices and push down to smash and flatten them. Set aside. Peel the ginger and cut it into 1-in (2.5-cm) pieces. Set aside.

In a straight-sided, stainless-steel or enamel-coated saucepan, 10 in (25 cm) in diameter, combine the water and sugar. Bring to a boil and simmer for 3 to 5 minutes to reduce into a light syrup.

Add the lemongrass, orange zest strips, and ginger to the saucepan with the syrup, remove from the heat, cover, and infuse for 1 hour. Add the grenadine syrup and bring the ingredients to a rolling boil. Remove the saucepan from the

heat, add the rhubarb, and use a rubber spatula to toss the rhubarb so that it is coated in the syrup. Cover and let sit to allow the hot liquid to poach the rhubarb. After 1 hour, remove the lid and check for doneness by poking the rhubarb with a paring knife or fork. The rhubarb should be just al dente and should resist the poke a little bit. If more cooking time is needed, return the saucepan to the stove and heat for 2 minutes, or until the liquid is simmering. Again remove the saucepan from the heat, cover, and let sit for 10 to 20 minutes, or until cooked through.

Cover the saucepan and let cool to room temperature. Place all the ingredients into an airtight container and put it into the refrigerator to chill completely. Serve cold over ice cream.

port & peppercorn glazed mission figs

There was an enormous Turkish fig tree in my grandmother's backyard in Istanbul; it looked like something out of *The Lord of the Rings* or a children's fantasy novel. I have very fond memories of being five years old and playing around that tree; I found copious amounts of sweet figs on the ground and on low-hanging branches and gorged myself on as many as could fit into my little stomach. By the time my mother called me in for dinner, I would have no appetite for the meal and was punished for not eating. This recipe is a classic French preparation of figs, but the fruit always reminds me of my childhood. I call for Black Mission figs here. Their red-purple color and rich natural flavor pairs extremely well with the deep, round, fruity aromas and flavors of the port wine. And the peppercorn gives your palate a kick at just the right moment. **YIELD: 20 FIG HALVES**

---

10 large, ripe Black Mission figs

75 g/¹/₄ cup plus 2 tbsp granulated sugar

150 g/²/₃ cup tawny port

3 g/1¹/₂ tsp whole black peppercorns

Remove the stems and cut the figs in half lengthwise with a paring knife. Set aside until ready to use.

Place a 10-in (25-cm) stainless-steel or enamel-coated saucepan over medium-high heat until just smoking. Add the sugar; it will melt right away and begin to caramelize and smoke. Immediately place the figs, cut-sides down, onto the caramelizing sugar. Reduce the heat to low and let the figs cook for 2 to 3 minutes. Do not toss. The figs will naturally release their own juices and melt the sugar.

Add the tawny port to the saucepan. Keep the saucepan over low heat until the caramel melts completely and begins to coat the figs. Add the black peppercorns. Use heat-resistant tongs to flip the figs over and cook for an additional 2 to 3 minutes. Remove the figs with tongs to a platter or baking sheet and keep warm. Return the pan to the stovetop and reduce the sauce over medium heat for 3 to 5 minutes, using a heat-resistant rubber spatula to stir and occasionally scrape the bottom to pull up all the caramel and peppercorn goodness that may be stuck there. The sauce should be deep purple, thickened, and velvety.

Put the warm figs, cut-sides up, on a beautiful platter and drizzle the port sauce over them. Serve immediately.

pluots baked in muscovado sugar & floral olive oil

I realize that I say this about a lot of fruits, but this time I really mean it: Pluots are my favorite fruit of all time. Not only do they have a cool name, but they are a great example of two good parents—plums and apricots—producing great offspring. All parents want to give the best of themselves to their children, and in this case it worked. Pluots retain the apricot's floral sweetness while showing off the juicy yet firm texture of the plum. I like to think of this preparation as the pluots' trip to the Caribbean. The sultry, dark flavors of the muscovado sugar and the floral notes of high-quality olive oil enhance the delicious perfection of the pluots even more. **YIELD: 8 SERVINGS**

---

455 g/1 lb Beauty Queen pluots

30 g/3 tbsp fragrant olive oil

Four 2-in (5-cm) strips orange zest (see page 110)

100 g/$\frac{1}{2}$ cup light muscovado sugar

2 g/$\frac{1}{2}$ tsp ground nutmeg

3 g/1 tsp Maldon sea salt

2 g/$\frac{1}{2}$ tsp ground Ceylon cinnamon (see Sources, page 216)

Preheat the oven to 375°F (190°C).

Use a paring knife to make a cut completely around the pit of a pluot; gently twist the two halves apart with your hands. Remove and discard the pit. Repeat with the remaining pluots. Set the prepared pluot halves in a 9-by-13-by-2-in (23-by-33-by-5-cm) baking pan or glass baking dish, cut-sides up. Pour the olive oil over the pluots, and scatter the orange zest strips over them.

In a small bowl, combine the muscovado sugar, nutmeg, sea salt, and cinnamon. Sprinkle this mixture over the pluots and toss to coat. Turn the pluots cut-sides down in the baking pan. Cover with aluminum foil and poke three to five holes into the foil to allow steam to escape while baking.

Place the pan into the oven and bake for 10 to 15 minutes, depending on the ripeness of the fruit. To check the doneness, remove the foil and look for the pluots to be releasing juices and bubbling up. Every 3 to 4 minutes, remove the foil and baste the pluots with the cooking liquid. When the pluots begin to release their juices, flip them over so their cut-sides are up, bake for another 3 to 4 minutes, baste once more, and remove from the oven. When the fruit is ready to be served, it should be soft and juicy on the inside and still hold its shape so its sweet flavors explode in your mouth. You don't want them to overcook and become mushy. Serve warm.

Sweet note: As stone fruit season comes to its end in late August, the pluots will often be firmer and won't release as much liquid while baking. You can help them along by sprinkling 2 tbsp water over them before baking.

roasted white peaches with olive oil, lavender honey & sea salt

I look forward to the Fourth of July, not because of childhood memories of barbecues and lawn darts, but because of peaches appearing on the market stands. Peaches are a sexy fruit. The perfect peach is effortless and sweet, like sitting outside among friends on a summer evening. If you're looking for a wonderful, simple dessert to bring to a summer gathering, look no further. **YIELD: 4 PEACH HALVES**

---

2 ripe white peaches

35 g/2 tbsp fragrant olive oil

Three 2-in (5-cm) strips orange zest (see page 110)

5 g/2 tsp Maldon sea salt

85 g/¼ cup lavender honey

4 fresh lemon verbena leaves

1 bunch of fennel flowers (optional)

Use a paring knife to make a cut completely around the peach pits; gently twist the halves apart with your hands. Remove and discard the pits. Set the peach halves in a baking dish, cut-sides up. Drizzle the olive oil over the peaches, scatter the orange zest strips over them, and sprinkle with the salt. Gently toss to coat the peaches.

Place the honey into a stainless-steel or enamel-coated saucepan, 12 in (30 cm) in diameter, over medium heat and slowly heat, 3 to 5 minutes. The honey will loosen and start to bubble and caramelize. Place 1 verbena leaf onto the cut side of each peach. Place the peaches, cut-sides down, into the pan. Cook over medium heat for 3 to 5 minutes, basting the peaches often with the warm honey. Flip the peaches over and cook for an additional 3 to 5 minutes, until they are tender and yielding when pierced with a knife. Remove the peaches from the pan and arrange them, cut-sides up, on a serving platter; sprinkle with fennel flowers, if desired, and serve immediately.

bosc pears roasted in caramel & indian spices

Hello fall! Pears are the first indication that summer is out and fall is around the corner as the last of the stone fruit leaves the market stands and pears and apples take over. In the Buddhist spirit of letting go of the past and embracing the present, I like to go full spice and fall spirit ahead. When I make this dry caramel, hearing the popping and crackling of the cinnamon and spices is extremely satisfying, and then the smell that fills the room is heavenly. In this preparation, you have the option to stop after the pears are poached, but I highly recommend that you take it to the next level in full, extravagant flavor and roast the pears as well. **YIELD: 3 TO 5 WHOLE POACHED PEARS**

1.6 kg/6$^1/_2$ cups water, plus 375 g/1$^1/_2$ cups

1 vanilla bean or 12 g/1 tbsp vanilla bean paste (see Sources, page 216)

425 g/2 cups plus 2 tbsp granulated sugar

6 cardamom pods

4 cinnamon sticks

5 black peppercorns

2 star anise pods

2 whole cloves

3 to 5 whole Bosc pears

In a large stainless-steel or enamel-coated saucepan, bring the 1.6 kg/6$^1/_2$ cups water to a boil. Once it is hot, set aside and keep warm. Split the vanilla bean in half lengthwise with a paring knife, and then use the knife to scrape the seeds from the pod. Reserve both the seeds and the pod.

In a separate 6- to 8-qt (5.5- to 7.5-L) stainless steel or enamel-coated saucepan, combine the sugar and remaining 375 g (1$^1/_2$ cups) water.

Cook the sugar-water until it is a dark amber color and begins to lightly smoke, creating a caramel, 365°F (185°C).

Remove the caramel from the heat. Use a heat-resistant rubber spatula to mix the cardamom pods, cinnamon sticks, black peppercorns, star anise pods, and cloves into the hot caramel. The intense heat of the caramel will release the essential oils of the woody spices. The

CONTINUED . . .

spices will pop and crackle when they first hit the caramel. Be brave and be prepared. Moving quickly so that the spices do not burn, pour one-third of the reserved hot water into the caramel mixture. Whisk to combine and then immediately pour in the rest of the hot water. The caramel will expand and release steam when you do this, so be cautious.

Return the saucepan to medium heat and bring the mixture to a boil. As the mixture heats up, use a whisk to stir the caramel to dissolve it into the water. If the caramel lumps up on the whisk, fear not; just keep stirring. The sugars will naturally melt into the hot syrup. Remove from the heat and place the scraped vanilla seeds and pod or vanilla bean paste into the caramel poaching liquid. Cover and let infuse for 2 to 3 hours, or overnight if you're feeling spicy.

Strain the poaching liquid into a bowl and discard the spices. Return the liquid to the saucepan, place it on the stove, and bring it back to a boil. While the liquid is heating up, peel the pears. Reduce the heat down to a low simmer. Place the pears into the syrup.

Poach the pears slowly and evenly until cooked through their centers, 20 to 45 minutes, depending on their ripeness (a more ripe pear will take less time). Cover the pears with a parchment paper lid and keep them evenly submerged while they are poaching. Alternatively, every once in a while use a wooden spoon to gently roll the pears in the liquid to ensure that they are evenly flavored and poached.

As the cooking time will vary depending on the ripeness of the pears, after 20 minutes, check the pears with a sharp paring knife to test doneness. It may take up to 45 minutes. When they are 85 percent done (the knife will slide easily into the pear but meet resistance in the center), remove them from the heat and allow the entire saucepan to cool to room temperature for 1 to 2 hours. This process will ensure that the pears poach beautifully to their center and will avoid overpoached, mushy pears.

Remove the pears from the poaching liquid with a slotted spoon, then cut the rounded bottom off to give each pear a flat sitting surface. Either serve or go on to roast them.

To roast the pears, preheat the oven to 350°F (180°C). Place the pears on a roasting pan or glass pan. Reduce the poaching liquid over high heat until it achieves a light, syrupy consistency. Pour the reduced poaching syrup over the pears while it is hot. Place the pears in the oven and roast for 7 to 12 minutes, basting with the syrup every few minutes to ensure nicely coated, glossy, and gorgeous pears.

Sweet Note: Unlike the other spices in this recipe, vanilla bean is not a dry spice, so it is infused into the liquid just at the end of cooking and during the resting period.

crystallized organic rose petals

This is one of those flights of fancy that is simple and worth it. The rose petals add a delicacy and a sparkle to any dessert dish that will make your guests feel honored and you feel like a 5-star pastry chef. Cooking with flowers has been a bit of an uphill battle in my professional career. In the United States, flowers in food are associated with overpowering perfume and soapy flavors. I beg to differ. When used in a delicate balance, most flowers, especially rose petals, are a divine culinary treat. Roses have a natural aroma and sweetness. This is definitely a seasonal bit of magic. Roses are available during the summer months, and you need to use organic, food-grade flowers. These petals add flair to any dessert—encourage your guests to eat them! Use them to garnish petits fours and wedding cakes. When you're working with the petals, go to a calm, meditative state, because the task takes delicate care and patience. **YIELD: 20 TO 30 PETALS**

---

20 g/4 egg whites

3 non-treated organic roses; choose your color

5 g/1½ tsp gelatin powder

200 to 400 g/1 to 2 cups granulated sugar

Set the egg whites out at least 2 hours before cooking to reach room temperature. Line a baking sheet with parchment paper or a Silpat.

Preheat the oven to 125°F (52°C). Hold a rose in one hand. With the other hand, grab and twist one rose petal at a time to gently pull off the petals. Repeat with the remaining roses. Fill a bowl with the rose petals and set aside.

Bring a saucepan of water to a low simmer. Place the egg whites in a medium bowl that can rest on top of the saucepan. Sprinkle with the gelatin powder and allow the gelatin to bloom for 5 minutes. Place the egg white mixture over the saucepan of simmering water to create a bain-marie. Warm the egg whites to 122°F (50°C). Turn up the heat slowly; it is important to keep the egg whites in a liquid state and to avoid cooking them. Remove the egg whites from the heat.

Use a clean, dry pastry brush to brush both sides of each rose petal with the warmed egg white wash. Pour the sugar into a separate medium bowl. Gently coat the rose petals with sugar, shake off the excess sugar, and lay the petals on the parchment paper–lined baking sheet. Repeat until all the petals are coated.

CONTINUED . . .

Place the rose petals in the oven for 20 to 30 minutes, or until the petals are dry. To check for doneness, allow a petal to cool for 3 minutes; it should crack easily between your fingers. Allow to cool for 1 hour on the countertop. Keep the rose petals in an airtight container in a cool, dry spot until ready to use as a garnish.

Sweet Note: Always use organically raised roses that have not been sprayed with pesticides. You can get culinary-grade rose petals from a culinary store, or from a friend's backyard. With the shimmering sugar coating, the rose petals will add beautiful color to most dishes. Play with the colors to find one that's right for you.

CHOCOLATE

As a pastry chef, I may push citrus scents and flower petals. It is perhaps my signature to wander the farmers' market at the end of the summer season and buy up flats of sun-candied fruits.

Some may say that I strive to bring something new to dessert. All these things may be true, but I still consider chocolate the king of desserts. It is ancient in its conquering and enthralling of the human race. In its raw form, chocolate has a bitter, citrus, seedlike flavor. Whoever created the earth gave us four elements, and I believe chocolate is the fifth—the element put here to remind us of the pleasures available to humankind.

If the world seems dark and dreary, and you're having a hard time remembering why you're pushing through each day, have a bite of chocolate, or better yet have a lot of chocolate. Let yourself remember that there is amazing beauty in the world, and it can be one bite.

The cacao is a tropical fruit, and the fruit that surrounds the bean has a sweet and juicy lychee-like flavor. The chocolate that we know and love today has to be fermented or roasted from its bean form into something sweeter. It is no wonder that the Aztecs considered it the food of the gods, an aphrodisiac, and a medicine.

They recognized it as the mood enhancer that Western scientists have since discovered it to be. In pre-Colombian times and up until the 1800s, chocolate was roasted, ground, and combined with water and spices to make a drink. It wasn't until 1879, when Rodolphe Lindt of Switzerland developed the technique of conching chocolate, that we had "melting chocolate" in a bar form. Since then, chocolate makers have been fine-tuning their craft by exposing the mixture to air, grinding it slowly, tempering it with cocoa butter, and other techniques.

Cacao beans grow in warm, tropical regions of the world, ranging from Africa, Central America, and the Caribbean to Hawaii, and many more. Once the beans are harvested, they are dried and then fermented, similar to the fermenting of grapes when making wine. Then they are roasted, similar to the roasting of coffee beans, before they start the next steps in production.

In March 2012, my friend Chloe, who is an editor in San Francisco, Frankie (the photographer for this book), and I met up with my childhood friend Rebecca in Paris, and to my delight we did nothing but tour the finest pâtisseries and eat to our sweet tooth's content. For days six and seven, we were graciously invited to visit the factory of Valrhona chocolatier. Nestled among centuries-old wineries in the Rhone Valley, Valrhona is a place where the chocolate makers are pure artists. They approach their craft with love and skill, creating flavor profiles through the strategic use of time, milk, and agitation. At the factory, I was simply awestruck when standing next to what must have been about a 450-lb (200-kg) stack of freshly roasted cacao beans, ready to

be pulverized. Although I'm not Aztec, I couldn't help but eat a good handful of the still-warm beans. Happily, our tour guide was polite and didn't intervene in this religious experience.

The founders of Valrhona actually picked their spot in the Rhone Valley with a distinct purpose. They wanted to start harnessing the craftsmanship and detail that the winemakers of the region had been perfecting for centuries for their new mission of producing chocolate. I have to admit, being there was a treat, pun intended. Walking up to their factory, I was embraced first not with a warm smile but with the thick, sweet smell of cocoa butter and roasting chocolate all around. It's entrancing. It's as though Willy Wonka is releasing chocolaty good vibes out into the world.

In touring the Valrhona facility, I came to understand why, although there may be a lot of chocolatiers in the world, only a small percentage of them are truly great. They have combined a skillful winemaker's technique with the pastry chef's attention to chemistry that at times borders on the obsessive. They never cut corners, and they study each new approach in detail before creating a new blend of chocolate. I met Vanessa Lemoine, who is one of the few existing *cacaotheques* in the world. The term actually means "cacao library," but she might as well have been Nikola Tesla explaining to me the theory behind electricity. Vanessa was a pure library of information of all things cocoa, and her knowledge could fill an entire book. Suffice it to say, it was a rare treat and one I will never forget.

To work with chocolate, it's important to know where it comes from. Like coffee and wine, chocolate that is sourced from a specific region will hold the flavors and profiles of that region. It is also important to choose a sustainably sourced chocolate, both for the land and for the people farming it. I was smitten to find a little bit of California in Tain-l'Hermitage, in that Valrhona actually works with very specific farms, developing relationships with them and helping them build communities. They do this not only for the sake of doing a good deed, but also to ensure a sustainable and consistent production of great cacao. As a proud San Franciscan, I found that this really hit my sweet spot!

It is in the grinding process that chocolate makers get a powdered substance, called chocolate liquor (sold as cocoa powder in stores), and the supple, fatty cocoa butter. Here's where the art comes in. Through the process of conching, the chocolate liquor is mixed with cocoa butter, milk solids, and sugar to create something wonderful. Conching can take anywhere from 5 hours to 3 days and, generally speaking, the longer the conching process, the higher the quality of the chocolate.

tempering chocolate

I learned to master everything chocolate from Luis Robledo-Richards at the Four Seasons in New York City. The man is a pure chocolate genius. When I started working with him, I was mesmerized by his calm and methodical demeanor toward pastry. Once I learned chocolate production with him, I realized that this is an absolutely necessary quality in any good pastry chef. Why do we refer to *tempering* chocolate? Because chocolate is a temperamental beast. One must be patient and work with it in an organized manner. Chocolate requires constant attention to the temperature, to the working environment, and to the amount of friction—or stirring—done during the tempering process.

I don't want to scare you—okay, maybe I do just a little bit, but only enough to ensure attention and love during the tempering process. The point of tempering chocolate is to have a glossy, snappy, delightful chocolate for dipping and coating treats. There is a lot of science in

chocolate work, and *especially* in tempering. I'll just say that tempering is the act of realigning the crystals in chocolate so that they can be melted, worked with, and then cooled back to a beautiful solid state. Chocolate crystals have five different stages of alignment, but only one of those stages leads to stable, glossy chocolate candies and coatings.

Basic chocolate tempering requires the chocolate to go through three stages: the melting temperature (113°F/45°C for dark, milk, and white chocolate), the crystallizing temperature (80 to 82°F/ 28 to 29°C for dark and milk chocolate; 79 to 81°F/26 to 27°C for white chocolate), and the working temperature (88 to 91°F/30 to 32°C for dark chocolate; 84 to 86°F/29 to 30°C for milk and white chocolate). The melting temperature is the temperature at which the cocoa butter melts and the chocolate reaches a fluid state. The crystallizing temperature refers to the cooler temperature at which the tempered chocolate starts to crystallize or harden. The working temperature refers to the working range, occurring when the chocolate is reheated slightly to a temperature at which it is fluid again but not out of temper. It is really essential to follow these temperatures accurately, as heating chocolate a few degrees above the working temperature will throw it "out of temper," causing it to bloom, at which point you will have to start over from step one. A basic digital thermometer is the perfect tool for achieving success in tempering chocolate, until you have mastered the "touch of the lip" test, which most pastry chefs use once they feel that they have tamed the art of chocolate.

In my pastry kitchen, I use the stone method to temper chocolate. This is a common method for chocolatiers and candy professionals to use. If you have access to a granite or marble slab and have the time to play around with some chocolate, this is a method worth learning. I always start out with chopped chocolate that is roughly the size of cherries. Most chocolate makers will sell their products in what's called *fèves*, or small pieces, which makes it easy to work with. First, I melt the chocolate over a bain-marie to its melting temperature. I then turn the chocolate out onto a marble slab and scrape and move it along the marble until it cools down to its crystallization temperature. I then reheat the cooled chocolate to its working temperature.

The other common method of tempering chocolate is the seeding method. This is a great method to use in your home kitchen. It involves melting two-thirds of the chocolate over a bain-marie to its melting temperature.

Alternatively, you can melt 250 g/8 oz of chocolate in a glass or plastic bowl in the microwave for 1 to 2 minutes, stirring every 30 seconds to ensure that you don't burn the chocolate. The reserved one-third is then added to the melted chocolate slowly, one piece at a time (remember, tempering is all about patience), while mixing with a rubber spatula until the chocolate is cooled to its crystallization temperature, and then it is quickly reheated to its working temperature.

Yet another method is what I like to refer to as the "cheating" method. You warm the chocolate to its melting temperature; fill another, larger bowl with cold water; and very carefully suspend the chocolate bowl in the cold water bath while stirring with a rubber spatula to bring it to its crystallization temperature. Finally, you warm it back up slightly to its working temperature. Take care not to get any, absolutely none, of the water into your melted chocolate, as it will start to emulsify into your chocolate, changing its texture completely. I suggest using a metal bowl for this method, as it's a better conductor of heat.

Chocolate that you purchase in the store has already been tempered, but if you are going to change its temperature, you must temper it again. Chocolate that is not tempered will bloom once it hardens. This happens when the cocoa butter or the sugar separates from the chocolate and forms streaks of white and gray over the surface as it sets. Untempered chocolate is safe to eat, but it won't look pretty, the taste will be unpleasant, and the texture will be significantly off when you bite into it. You will not have the distinct pleasure of feeling it melt on your tongue.

chocolate decorations

Chocolate and plastic work really well together. Tempered chocolate that is spread on a plastic surface, or into a bonbon mold, will have a glossy, shiny surface when it crystallizes. You can find textured plastic sheets made for chocolate work in specialty cooking stores or online. You can also go to the hardware store and get any plastic sheets with texture, including covers for fluorescent lighting, clean them well, and use them as your chocolate molds. Any texture will do, as long as the "mold" is made of hard plastic.

For this preparation, I use two half-sheets of textured plastic acetate. Use a wet towel to dampen the workspace (so your acetate doesn't slide as you work with the chocolate), and place one acetate sheet on the workspace. Don't get the workspace too wet; you don't want water droplets to fall into your chocolate.

Temper 250 g/8 oz of 55% to 72% dark chocolate (see page 150). Pour 200 g/1 cup tempered chocolate across the top third of the plastic and immediately use a large offset spatula to spread the chocolate down and across the acetate, creating an even layer. It is important to work quickly to spread the chocolate; as time passes it will start to set and crystallize. You want a nice, even sheet before that happens. Keep in mind that as chocolate sets, it wants to naturally curve upward; so if you want a really flat surface, place another acetate sheet, followed by a baking sheet, directly on top as it starts to harden. The small amount of weight will ensure that your chocolate garnishes remain flat.

To use the decorations as chocolate shards, allow the chocolate to crystallize on the plastic overnight, then gently peel the acetate off. Reserve the acetate to use again. Use clean hands to gently break the chocolate into shards and rough squares for garnishing desserts.

To create cut-out decorations, begin working with the chocolate once the layer is even and the chocolate has set to a semifirm consistency. This will take a few minutes, depending on the temperature of the room you are working in. The chocolate should be tacky to the touch but no longer melted. Use a ring mold or round cookie cutter and press it into the chocolate, using a twisting motion to achieve a clean, even cut. It's important to do this quickly before the sheet sets. To make half-moons, cut a circle and then lift the cutter and move it over so that it overlaps the first circle by about a third; then press and twist again. Leave the chocolate on the plastic to crystallize overnight. Once the chocolate is fully set, flip the plastic sheet over, gently peel off the plastic, and then carefully pull the cutouts apart, using your thumb and forefingers as a guide on the cut lines. Save any extra pieces to temper again or to use in a different recipe—there's no need for them to go to waste.

emulsify my love!

Emulsification! I am a pastry nerd, through and through. That's why chocolate emulsification gets me excited every time I do a demo. It speaks to the core of why pastry is built on science and knowledge, not myth. Understanding and mastering this one very simple technique will help you tremendously in most chocolate recipes and beyond. Chocolate emulsion is the foundation for most chocolate recipes, including ganache, *crémeux*, and custards. If you've ever had a chocolate dessert separate on you, chances are good this technique will help you.

Any culinary emulsion is the mixing of two different liquids, a fat and a water, to create one consistent body. Consider what happens when you begin to make vinaigrette: The vinegar sits on top of the oil; they are two completely separate bodies. Add friction—shake it up—and the two will come together and hold a tantalizing silkiness for about 30 seconds, until they settle back into two separate bodies. Add an emulsifier, such as mustard or egg yolk, and friction, and the two will combine and hold together much longer.

A chocolate emulsion is based on the same principle. It is the combining of a fat, such as cocoa butter, with a liquid, such as cream, fruit purée, or other complementary liquid. We add friction and heat to these two elements through the use of a rubber spatula or an immersion blender and a bain-marie. Chocolate emulsions happen above 94°F (34.5°C), and are best between 94° and 122°F (35° and 50°C).

I will first encourage you not to get discouraged in reading through this chapter. The art of working with chocolate can

seem impossible to master. But as with anything in life, put in the effort, and you will master it. It may seem as though there are a lot of variables and ratios, but if you follow the basic procedure in the ganache section that follows, and observe as you follow the steps, the process will become very clear to you.

Different types of chocolate have different amounts of cocoa butter, and these differences affect the melting point as well as the temperature at which it emulsifies. Dark chocolate contains less cocoa butter and thus emulsifies at a lower temperature than milk chocolate or white chocolate. When you're following a recipe, be sure to purchase chocolate with the recommended percentage of cacao.

The cocoa butter in chocolate will melt when heated, but the solids in it, be they cocoa solids, sugar, or milk solids, will burn if overheated, which is why each type of chocolate has a "melting" temperature, at which it's fluid but not burnt. Keep a damp kitchen towel next to the bain-marie as you work; when the chocolate begins to heat up too much, move the bowl over and rest it on the towel. The towel will keep the bowl from slipping as you continue to add friction. Heat the chocolate and the liquid separately to between 94° and 104°F (35° and 40°C) before bringing them together.

The ratio of cocoa butter to the complementary liquid is based on the actual water content of the liquid being used. For example, milk has more water content than heavy cream, and passion fruit purée has more water by nature than raspberry purée, which will have more fruit solids and pectin. Therefore, it's not ideal to substitute equal amounts of ingredients as you play around with recipes. It's important to understand not only how they affect flavor but also how their structure and chemistry will affect the texture.

In many of the cooking classes I've taught over the last few years, I share a metaphor for the trials and tribulations of chocolate emulsion. Chocolate and cream are like a big group of relatives who have come together for a holiday meal. In the beginning they are cold, shy, and timid about mixing together. Once you start passing around the gin martinis (heat), everyone starts to relax and melt down a bit; give them some delicious food (friction) and keep the drinks flowing. Before you know it, everyone is mixing together, laughing, and becoming a homogenous group—they are a family again.

Chocolate emulsions are no different. Cold chocolate and cream are two completely different bodies that have nothing to do with each other. Heat them up and add the right amount of friction, and they come together to create a beautiful, silky, delicious chocolate creation. Chocolate ganache or *crémeux*, once emulsified, should look like shiny chocolate mayonnaise.

MAKING GANACHE

A ganache is the most basic chocolate emulsion, and at the same time it is one of the most sultry, rich, and enjoyable experiences your mouth can have. A ganache has the two basic elements of an emulsion: the liquid, a mixture of heavy cream and invert sugar, and fat, in the form of chopped chocolate and sometimes butter. Making a ganache is an act of simple and precise love. Get to know this lovely form of chocolate, and you'll have a silky, gorgeous cake topping in your back pocket. I'm including the basic steps for making a ganache here so that you can see how simple it really is. Play with different ratios of chocolate to cream, as well as different types of chocolate, to find your personal favorite recipe.

When you create a *crémeux* (see page 161), you're using the same technique; the addition of cooked eggs gives the final product a thicker body—flavor with texture.

1. In a stainless-steel saucepan, bring cream and sugar to a boil, to ensure that they are combined and the sugar is dissolved. Turn off the heat and set aside. Meanwhile, melt your chopped chocolate in a bowl over a bain-marie to its melting point (see page 150).

2. Gently pour half of the warm cream mixture over the melted chocolate. Make friction your friend—the greater the friction, the more silky and completely combined the ganache. Mix by hand with a rubber spatula, starting from the center of the bowl outward, and mix the two bodies together until they start to come together. This is called a *pre-emulsion*. The mixture will thicken and may separate and come together, then separate and come together again. Don't worry; be fearless and press on. The elements are just getting to know each other as the melted cocoa butter saturates.

3. Pour the remainder of the warm cream mixture into the chocolate mixture and keep mixing (adding friction). A thick, shiny, consistent emulsion will form. At this point, if you have a handheld immersion blender, put it into your ganache and tap it at the bottom of the bowl several times to release the air. I find that it works best if you hold the blender at a 30-degree angle and move the bowl in a circular motion as you blend. This will give you a really gorgeous emulsion, and your ganache should resemble a dark and shiny mayonnaise. Very sexy indeed!

CONTINUED . . .

4. Now your ganache is finished, but if you are adding butter to make truffles or molded bonbons, there is one very important thing to keep in mind. Wait until your ganache cools to between 95° to 104°F (35° to 40°C) before blending in the butter. If you blend the butter while the ganache is very hot, the butter will melt, and the water in the butter will separate. When it sets and crystallizes as it cools, it will have a grainy texture rather than the creamy texture you are aiming for.

Sweet Note: A ganache is one of the most fundamental recipes in a baker's repertoire. You can make it in large batches by preparing it through step 3. Once the cream is emulsified, pour the ganache into smaller airtight containers and keep in your freezer for up to 3 months. When ready for use, just thaw it in the microwave and emulsify with a handheld blender to bring it back to a silky texture. Then add the butter, if using, following step 4.

earl grey tea–infused chocolate truffles

I love tea! I'm not sure if it's my Turkish heritage or my hero worship of Captain Jean-Luc Picard, but I've always loved tea, and through the years Earl Grey has remained my favorite. It is the king of teas. It harnesses the dark, bitter flavors of a great black tea, while the bergamot oil that gives Earl Grey its distinct flavor imparts the fruity and citrusy notes that make this tea so complex and wonderful. What happens when you marry this lovely flavor with the complexities of dark and milk chocolate and butter? I created these truffles to answer that question. The basic truffle recipe is just a ganache that has butter added to it, and it can be infused with various flavors. I invite you to experience the divine. **YIELD: 50 TRUFFLES**

---

80 g/¹/₃ cup unsalted butter

370 g/13 oz 66% to 70% dark chocolate

480 g/2 cups heavy cream, plus more to replenish after steeping

20 g/1 tbsp plus 1 tsp Earl Grey tea leaves

75 g/3 tbsp plus 2 tsp corn syrup or glucose syrup (see Sources, page 216)

150 g/2 cups unsweetened cocoa powder

Cut the butter into ¹/₂-in (12-mm) chunks and set it on the counter about 2 hours before cooking to allow it to come to room temperature.

In a large stainless-steel or glass bowl, melt the chocolate over a saucepan of simmering water. Alternatively, melt the chocolate in the microwave on medium power for about 45 seconds, or until melted. Stir the chocolate every 20 seconds with a rubber spatula so that it doesn't burn. Keep warm.

In a medium stainless-steel or enamel-coated saucepan, over medium heat, bring the heavy cream to a boil. Whisk the tea leaves into the hot cream. Remove from the heat. Cover the saucepan and let steep for 7 to 8 minutes.

Strain the cream through a fine-mesh sieve or cheesecloth and discard the tea leaves. Add more fresh heavy cream to bring it back to the original volume (the tea leaves will have soaked some up). Clean out the saucepan to remove any leftover tea leaves. Return the strained cream to the clean saucepan, add the corn syrup, and bring it back to a boil.

Place the bowl of melted chocolate on the countertop with a towel underneath so it doesn't shift around when mixing. Pour half of the infused cream over the melted chocolate and begin to emulsify with a rubber spatula. Stir quickly at first to begin the emulsification process (see page 154). Pour in the remainder

CONTINUED . . .

of the cream and continue mixing to emulsify the mixture. Finish by mixing with a handheld blender to obtain a silky emulsion. Set the ganache in a cool space on the countertop and allow it to cool to 95° to 104°F (35° to 40°C).

Add the butter to the ganache. Use the handheld blender to emulsify the mixture completely, until all the butter is incorporated and the mixture looks like a silky, thick chocolate mayonnaise.

Place a layer of plastic wrap directly on the surface of the ganache to prevent a skin from forming. Keep at room temperature overnight to cool and crystallize. The ganache can be made in advance and held in the refrigerator in an airtight container for up to 5 days. When ready to create the truffles, take the ganache out of the refrigerator 2 to 3 hours before using and set it on the countertop to allow it to come to room temperature.

Sift the cocoa powder into a large, shallow bowl; line a baking sheet with parchment paper. Use a small #60 scoop to make $1/2$-in (12-mm) balls of the ganache. Roll each ball in your hands (powder-free latex gloves work great for this process) until rounded and truffle shaped. Place a few truffles into the cocoa powder and roll them around to coat, shake off excess powder by tossing them in a fine-mesh sieve, and then transfer them to the prepared baking sheet. Work in small batches so the truffles do not stick to each other in the powder.

Pile the truffles in a glass bowl and enjoy. The truffles can be stored in an airtight container at room temperature for up to 1 week. Roll in fresh cocoa powder before serving.

Sweet Note: Truffles are named after a mushroom that is found in the mud by pigs or dogs trained for the scent. Keep this fact in mind when forming the balls; it is okay if they are oddly shaped and a little lumpy. The chocolate truffle betrays a pastry chef's envy of a savory chef's upscale ingredients. Savory black truffles are known for their aroma and the flavor they bring to dishes.

dark chocolate crémeux

A creamy, luscious, and rich chocolate emulsion, *crémeux* rises above mousses and pastry creams to become its own incredible combination of cream and chocolate. A good *crémeux* knows where it stands. **YIELD: 4½ CUPS (1 L)**

345 g/12.5 oz Valrhona Guanaja 70% dark chocolate, broken into pieces

120 g/6 egg yolks

50 g/¼ cup granulated sugar

240 g/1 cup heavy cream

240 g/1 cup whole milk

In a medium stainless-steel or glass bowl, melt the chocolate over a saucepan of simmering water. Alternatively, melt the chocolate in the microwave on medium power for about 45 seconds, or until melted. Stir the chocolate every 20 seconds with a rubber spatula so that it doesn't burn. Keep warm.

Fill a large bowl halfway with ice and then add cold water to almost cover. Make sure the water won't spill out when the bowl of custard is placed into the ice bath.

In a separate small bowl, combine the egg yolks and sugar; whisk to break up the yolks and dissolve the sugar. Bring the heavy cream and milk to a boil in a medium stainless-steel or enamel-coated saucepan. To heat up the egg yolks slowly, add ¼ cup (60 ml) of the cream to the egg yolk mixture, whisking to combine. This method will keep the egg yolks from cooking when you add them to the hot cream.

Add the warmed egg yolk mixture to the cream mixture by slowly pouring it into the cream mixture while whisking. Once the egg yolk mixture is fully incorporated, use a rubber spatula to stir the mixture so that it does not stick to the bottom of the saucepan. Clean the sides of the saucepan with the rubber spatula as you're cooking. Bring the mixture to 180°F (82°C). Strain through a fine-mesh sieve into a separate, medium bowl.

Pour half of the hot custard over the melted chocolate and use a heat-resistant rubber spatula to stir, quickly at first to begin to emulsify the custard and chocolate (see page 154). Pour in the remainder of the custard and continue mixing. Use a handheld blender to completely emulsify the mixture. You will have a glossy chocolate custard that should resemble a chocolate mayonnaise.

Place a layer of plastic wrap directly on the surface of the custard to prevent a skin from forming. Place the bowl of custard into the ice bath; chill to room temperature. Cover completely and chill in the refrigerator overnight.

Chocolate *crémeux* can be prepared up to 5 days in advance. When ready to serve, use a pastry bag to pipe the cold *crémeux* into stemless wineglasses or serving bowls.

mendiants with candied ginger, hazelnut, pistachio & dried sour cherry

A *mendiant* is a classic French chocolate candy, usually coin-shaped or circular. I always find myself making these little chocolate morsels at Christmastime, and as I'm doing so I wonder why I don't make them throughout the year. This is a simple way to make an elegant chocolate treat. The dried fruits pair beautifully with the sweetness and bitterness of milk chocolate, elevating its complex flavors. Pistachios add a beautiful soft crunch and color. Once you've mastered tempering chocolate, you'll find these are really fun to make in your kitchen. Taking a box of these gorgeous morsels to a gathering or sending them as a gift is a sure way to make people happy.

YIELD: ABOUT 15 PIECES

---

15 whole natural, green pistachios, shelled

8 whole natural, raw hazelnuts, halved

500 g/1¼ lb 33% to 40% milk chocolate

30 dried sour cherries

15 strips candied ginger, 1 in (2.5 cm) long

1 sheet gold leaf (optional)

SPECIAL EQUIPMENT:
One 12-by-16-in (30-by-40-cm) sheet of plastic acetate or parchment paper

---

CONTINUED . . .

Preheat the oven to 200°F (95°C). Spread the pistachios and hazelnuts on a baking sheet and roast for approximately 10 minutes. The pistachios should remain naturally green in color, and all the nuts will dry out and have a bit more crunch.

Temper the milk chocolate (see page 150). Line a baking sheet with the acetate. Fit a piping bag with a #3 plain piping tip and close the mouth of the piping bag just above the tip using a binder clip, so that when you pour the tempered chocolate into the piping bag, it won't come out. Place all the chocolate into the piping bag. Remove the binder clip and immediately pipe small dollops of milk chocolate, 1 in (2.5 cm) in diameter, onto the acetate until you run out of chocolate. Pick up the baking sheet and gently tap it against a counter to flatten the chocolate into thin disks, about 1½ in (4 cm) in diameter. Work quickly to put one piece of candied ginger, two sour cherries, a pistachio, and half a hazelnut on top of each chocolate disk before it sets and while it still has a lot of give to it. Press gently onto each addition so that it will be held in the chocolate. Place a small piece of gold leaf onto an edge of each chocolate, if desired.

Set the baking sheet in a cool, dry place and allow the chocolate to crystallize for a minimum of 6 hours, preferably overnight. If you're working in a very hot kitchen, above 86°F (30°C), and the chocolate won't crystallize, place it in the refrigerator for 15 minutes (do this only if necessary; the chocolate may get condensation on it, and you'll lose your glossy finish), and then place at room temperature.

Once the chocolate is completely crystallized, remove the pieces from the acetate sheet and store them in a cool, dry place for up to 1 month.

chocolate-covered macadamia nut dragées

This was one of the first steps in my chocolate apprenticeship with Chef Luis Robledo-Richards at the Four Seasons. He insisted that working with this simple form of tempered chocolate would build my foundation of chocolate work. I owe that man a debt of gratitude, and I continue to make and sell these nuts at Tout Sweet. This is an excellent entry to chocolate work, and you'll end up with incredibly tasty little morsels that you can't help but pop into your mouth. **YIELD: 7 CUPS (1.5 KG)**

---

650 g/2 cups cocoa powder

1 kg/7 cups macadamia nuts

200 g/7 oz 64% to 78% dark chocolate, preferably Valrhona

80 g/¹⁄₄ cup corn syrup

200 g/1 cup granulated sugar

Preheat the oven to 350°F (180°C). Line a rimmed baking sheet with parchment paper and set aside. Sift the cocoa powder into a shallow bowl and set aside. Place the macadamia nuts in a large mixing bowl.

Break the dark chocolate into pieces and place it in a large stainless-steel or glass bowl. While you start the process of caramelizing your macadamias, melt the chocolate over a saucepan of simmering water. Alternatively, microwave on low power for about 2 minutes, or until melted. Keep the heat low and stir the chocolate every 20 seconds with a rubber spatula so that it doesn't burn.

Microwave the corn syrup for about 15 seconds so that it is more liquid, or warm it in a small saucepan over very low heat for 3 to 5 minutes. Pour the corn syrup over the nuts and use a rubber spatula to toss gently and coat the nuts. Sprinkle the sugar on top of the nuts; toss to evenly coat. The nuts should be lightly coated with a sandy texture. Think of the beaches in Maui. Pour them onto the parchment paper–lined baking sheet and spread evenly.

Roast the nuts in the oven, tossing them every 3 to 5 minutes to achieve a golden brown caramel color all over each nut; roast for 10 to 15 minutes, or until the nuts are evenly golden. Meanwhile, clean and dry the bowl they were tossed in.

CONTINUED . . .

Remove the baking sheet from the oven and set it on a countertop to cool completely. Once the nuts are cool to the touch, return them to their original bowl. Cover with the melted chocolate and toss them around to cool the melted chocolate so it begins to harden over the individual nuts. (It's important that the covered nuts be a little tacky to the touch but not wet with melted chocolate, as the melted chocolate will soak up too much cocoa powder, making it impossible to achieve an even coat and causing the dragées to be bitter.)

Working with five to ten nuts at a time, drop them into the reserved cocoa powder. Take your time and don't overfill the bowl, to avoid having the nuts stick together. Roll them in the cocoa powder and transfer to a sifter or fine-mesh sieve. Shake off the excess cocoa powder. You will have beautiful, individually coated nuts. I suggest sifting the nuts a second time through a colander to get rid of bigger clumps of powder and achieve an even coating of cocoa powder all over each nut.

Store in an airtight container in a cool, dry place for up to 1 month.

double molten chocolate cake

This recipe reflects the battle between my professional ego and my personal inner cravings. As a chef, I want desperately to move on from the molten—or lava—chocolate cake movement that swept the pastry world sometime in the 1980s and just won't go away. As a chocolate and cake addict, though, I want to hold on and never let go. Each time we make this in the kitchen, my cooks are sure to find me scooping up the remnants of a broken, oozing cake—it is just so good! Because you are aiming for molten softness in the center, there will likely be one fallen soldier in each batch of cakes, but I doubt it will go to waste! **YIELD: 10 INDIVIDUAL CAKES**

---

300 g/6 eggs

80 g/^{2}/$_3$ cup all-purpose flour

250 g/1^1/$_4$ cups granulated sugar

180 g/^{3}/$_4$ cup unsalted butter

190 g/6^3/$_4$ oz chopped 70% dark chocolate

Set the eggs out 1 hour ahead of time to come to room temperature; this is essential so that the chocolate does not seize. Sift the flour over parchment paper and set aside.

Combine the eggs and sugar in a stand mixer fitted with the whisk attachment. Whisk the mixture to completely combine and bring to the thick ribbon stage; it will be a pale yellow color and will have tripled in size.

Combine the butter and chocolate in a medium stainless-steel or glass bowl. Bring a saucepan of water to a medium simmer and place the bowl over the simmering water. Stir with a heat-resistant rubber spatula until the chocolate and butter are melted. Remove from the heat when the mixture is at 122°F (50°C).

Gently fold the warm, not hot, chocolate mixture into the whipped eggs and sugar. Use a rubber spatula to fully mix and evenly combine. Add the sifted flour to the mixture and fold it in to fully combine. Be sure there are no lumps of flour. Place plastic wrap directly onto the surface of the batter to fully cover it and put the bowl in the refrigerator for 1 hour, or up to 5 days.

Preheat the oven to 350°F (180°C). Line a baking sheet with parchment paper. Prepare ten ring molds, 3 in (7.5 cm) in diameter and 2 in (5 cm) tall, by coating the inside with cooking spray, lining the molds with 3-in- (7.5-cm-) wide strips of parchment paper, and then coating the parchment paper again with cooking spray. The parchment will extend 1 in (2.5 cm) above the tops of the molds. Place the molds on the prepared baking sheet.

Pipe or spoon 110 g/$\frac{1}{2}$ cup of cake batter into each ring mold. You can do this by putting the baking sheet on top of your electronic scale as you fill the molds, to make sure you have the same amount in each mold. Alternatively, pipe them $\frac{1}{2}$ in (12 mm) below the top of the ring mold, leaving 1$\frac{1}{2}$ in (4 cm) of parchment exposed at the top. The molds should be about three-quarters full. Bake for 10 minutes, then rotate the baking sheet 180 degrees and bake for another 5 to 7 minutes, or until the cakes puff up and begin to pull away from the molds but still have a soft and jiggly spot in the center about the size of a nickel. Do not overbake these treats, or they will start to shrink and become dry and fudgelike. Place the baking sheet on a cooling rack and cool completely, 15 minutes, before you fuss with them any further. Carefully remove the ring molds; if necessary, gently push the cakes up while holding the ring mold to release them. Gently peel off the parchment paper, taking care not to tear the cakes. When ready to serve, return the unmolded cakes to the oven 350°F (180°C) for 5 to 7 minutes, until the center is warm again, but without cooking them any further. Serve hot.

Sweet Note: This is a really decadent dessert. Even if you don't go the to the extreme, as I suggest on page 212, this cake still begs for something creamy and refreshing, like a vanilla bean ice cream or even a tall glass of organic milk.

bittersweet flourless chocolate cake

I love this cake for many reasons, the most important of which is that it is a gluten-free dessert created long before the wheat-free and gluten-free craze hit the world. This is simply a group of great ingredients that comes together to become a great cake. This cake has a rich chocolate flavor. It becomes cakey and rich from the egg yolks combined with the folded-in French meringue and finishes with a very moist texture. Making this cake requires a good amount of technique and painstaking work, but it is well worth it. If you want to use this to make a layered cake, bake it in a shallow 18-by-26-in (46-by-66-cm) baking pan and then cut out the cake circles with a ring mold. It is a very delicate, intensely moist cake and, unlike a traditional flour-based cake, it can't be baked in a round cake pan and sliced horizontally through the center to create layers, so you must bake it at the thickness of the layers that you will use.

YIELD: ONE 9-BY-13-IN (23-BY-33-CM) CAKE

---

500 g/2^1/$_2$ cups granulated sugar

220 g/11 egg yolks at room temperature

330 g/11 egg whites at room temperature

5 g/1 tsp fresh lemon juice

100 g/1^1/$_4$ cups cocoa powder

Preheat the oven to 375°F (190°C). Line the bottom of a 9-by-13-by-2-in (23-by-33-by-5-cm) baking pan with parchment paper.

Use a stand mixer with the whisk attachment to combine 350 g/1^3/$_4$ cups of the sugar and all of the egg yolks. Whisk on high speed until the mixture reaches the pale ribbon stage, at which point it will have tripled in size and have pale yellow peaks. You don't need to be on high alert here; you can't overwhip the mixture. Once mixed, use a rubber spatula to gently transfer the mixture to a large bowl; minimum 4 qt (3.8 L).

Wash, rinse, and dry the whisk attachment and mixer bowl. Add the egg whites to the mixing bowl with the whisk attachment, then add the lemon juice. Begin whipping on medium speed to make a meringue. At this point, pay attention; you don't want to overwhip the egg whites (see page 74). Slow the speed when the mixture has nearly doubled in size and very soft peaks begin to form; gradually add the remaining 150 g/^{3}/$_4$ cup sugar and whisk to combine. Whisk the meringue until glossy, 1 to 2 minutes. Use a rubber spatula to gently fold the meringue into the egg yolk mixture. Do not deflate the mixture.

Sift the cocoa powder over the egg mixture; use a rubber spatula to gently fold the mixture until the cocoa powder is just incorporated into the eggs. Take care not to overmix the cake batter and don't let it deflate. Treat it like a friend . . . very gently.

Gently pour the batter into the parchment paper–lined baking pan. Use an offset spatula to spread it evenly. Bake for 9 minutes. Rotate the pan 180 degrees and bake for another 3 to 5 minutes, or until the cake lightly bounces back to the touch.

Sweet Note: Baking chocolate cakes tends to be tricky, since you can't tell when the golden brown color is developing, so be attentive and rely on touch more than eyesight.

dark chocolate soufflé

The chocolate soufflé is a standard in the pastry chef's kitchen, and while myth and legend have grown up around the delicacy and impossibility of the soufflé, success is much easier than you think. The balance of lightness and decadence makes this a guaranteed crowd pleaser—and delivering a beautifully puffed soufflé to the table is sure to garner *oohs* and *aahs*. The secret about chocolate soufflés is that the cocoa butter helps the meringue to set and stabilize, which means that this batter can be made up to 3 hours in advance and still reach incredible heights. There's no need to tell your guests this—just come out of your kitchen with a beautiful soufflé, and accept the compliments. **YIELD: 12 SERVINGS**

---

330 g/11 egg whites

40 g/2 egg yolks

Butter for greasing the ramekins

200 g/1 cup granulated sugar

400 g/14 oz 70% dark chocolate; preferably Valrhona

3 g/¹/₂ tsp lemon juice

Set the egg whites and yolks on the countertop for 1 hour to come to room temperature. Preheat the oven to 375°F (190°C).

Coat twelve 6- to 8-oz (180- to 240-ml) ramekins with a thin layer of butter, then pour 1 tsp of the sugar into each butter-coated ramekin and swirl to coat the entire dish with sugar. Shake out the excess sugar.

Bring a saucepan of water to a simmer. Place a large stainless-steel or glass bowl over the saucepan to create a bain-marie. Put the chocolate in the bowl and melt it, stirring occasionally. Turn off the heat and keep the chocolate warm over the bain-marie.

Use a stand mixer with a whisk attachment to combine the egg whites, lemon juice, and

remaining 150 g/³/₄ cup sugar. Whisk to shiny, full peaks (see page 74). While the meringue is being whisked, pour the egg yolks into a small bowl. Add ¹/₄ cup (60 ml) of the chocolate to the yolks, then add this mixture to the chocolate and mix evenly. The chocolate will want to set up, so keep it warm over the bain-marie and keep mixing.

As soon as the meringue is whipped, fold one-third into the chocolate mixture to lighten up the mixture. Gently add another third of the meringue to the chocolate mixture and fold; then add the rest of the meringue. Use a rubber spatula to fold the chocolate and meringue together. It is very important to be delicate and gently fold the batter, to avoid deflating it.

CONTINUED . . .

Use a soup spoon to gently spoon $^3/_4$ cup (180 ml) of the soufflé batter into each sugar-coated ramekin, until each ramekin is filled to $^1/_4$ in (6 mm) below the rim. Set the ramekins on a baking sheet and place the baking sheet in the oven. Immediately close the oven door to avoid lowering the heat. Bake the soufflés for 7 to 10 minutes, until they have risen about $1^1/_2$ in (4 cm) above the tops of the ramekins. It is very important to keep the oven door closed so as not to drop the oven temperature and cause the soufflés to fall. Serve immediately.

Sweet Note: The great thing about these soufflés is that the batter can be prepared up to 3 hours in advance, spooned into the ramekins, and held in a cool area (not the refrigerator), so they can be baked just before serving.

spanish hot chocolate with aztec spices & pasilla chile

What could be better on a cold winter day than a cup of steaming hot chocolate? History says that the Aztecs were drinking a chocolate drink when the conquistadors stumbled upon them. I like to imagine some enterprising ancient chocolatier pulling chile and cinnamon from the forest to simmer into the chocolate and give the tribe a wake-up call. While my history may be a bit fantastical, this drink will wake up the senses and warm the bones. **YIELD: 6 SERVINGS**

---

190 g/6³/₄ oz 70% dark chocolate, broken into pieces, plus more for shaving over the top

1 vanilla bean or 12 g/1 tbsp vanilla bean paste (see Sources, page 216)

1 dried pasilla chile

One 4-in (10-cm) cinnamon stick

640 g/2³/₄ cups plus 1 tbsp whole milk

120 g/¹/₂ cup heavy cream

60 g/3 tbsp corn syrup

Grated zest of 1 orange (see page 110)

150 g/1 cup Vanilla Bean Chantilly (page 81) for topping

Preheat the oven to 325°F (165°C). Place the chocolate pieces in a stainless-steel or glass 2- to 3-qt (2- to 2.8-L) bowl, and set aside. Split the vanilla bean in half lengthwise with a paring knife, and then use the knife to scrape the seeds from the pod. Reserve both the seeds and the pod.

Split the dried pasilla chile in half and place it on a baking sheet. Add the cinnamon stick to the baking sheet. Toast in the oven for 3 to 5 minutes to release the essential oils. Keep your eyes on the spices and remove the cinnamon and chile from the oven as they start to toast; do not let them burn.

Meanwhile, in a 2-qt (2-L) stainless-steel or enamel-coated saucepan, bring the milk, cream, and corn syrup to a boil. Add the toasted cinnamon stick and chile, reserved vanilla pod and seeds or vanilla bean paste, and orange zest to the saucepan. Cover, remove from the heat, and let steep for 1 hour. Once it has steeped, use a handheld blender to blend the mixture,

CONTINUED . . .

breaking up the chile as well as the cinnamon stick and vanilla pod. This may seem crazy, but it really draws delicious flavor out of the spices. The mixture will turn a brick-orange color as the pasilla releases its color and flavor.

Bring the mixture gently back to a quick boil and strain the milk through a fine-mesh sieve over the bowl of chocolate pieces. Whisk or use a handheld blender until the chocolate is incorporated and the mixture becomes supple and emulsified.

Pour the hot chocolate into mugs and top with chantilly and chocolate shavings. Serve hot. Alternatively, the hot chocolate can be cooled and stored in an airtight container in the refrigerator for up to 3 days. Stir with a rubber spatula as you gently reheat it on the stovetop.

three-minute chocolate sauce

My addiction to ice cream knows no bounds. A pint of store-bought ice cream has been my dinner on more than one occasion. As a young pastry cook in New York City, I lived in a tiny apartment with a roommate. Our oven was storage space, and there was no pantry to speak of. We decided one night to make ice cream sundaes and pulled all the sweet ingredients we could find out of the cupboard. In my mind, there is no sundae without the chocolate sauce, and it was some kind of a miracle that these three ingredients were in the apartment. I mixed them together, put the bowl in the microwave for 3 minutes, and voilà! A silky, rich chocolate sauce that made me and my roommate feel like kids for one night. **YIELD: 1¼ CUPS (300 ML)**

---

125 g/4.4 oz 64% to 72% dark chocolate

160 g/²/₃ cup half-and-half

15g/1 tbsp granulated sugar

Place the chocolate, half-and-half, and sugar in a glass or plastic bowl. In a microwave, on medium power, cook the mixture to melt the chocolate and combine. This should take about 3 minutes; stir the mixture every 15 to 20 seconds so the chocolate doesn't burn. Remove from the microwave when fully melted. If a microwave is not available, combine all the ingredients in a stainless-steel or glass bowl and place over a saucepan of gently simmering water. Gently melt the chocolate while stirring with a rubber spatula, 3 to 5 minutes. Use a handheld blender to incorporate the ingredients and create a silky, sexy sauce. Use immediately.

ALCHEMY

the luscious raspberry [184]
creamy mascarpone bavarian, citrus-scented almond génoise cake,
salty hazelnut & brown sugar crumble, baked berry meringue kisses,
organic raspberries

lavender pavlovas [186]
with lychee, raspberries, and vanilla bean chantilly

negroni creamsicle [188]
citrus-scented panna cotta; blood orange, grapefruit & campari gelée;
citrus suprêmes; lime zest

strawberry-lime sorbet vacherin [190]
with lemongrass poached rhubarb, lemongrass & ginger ice cream,
baked berry meringue kisses, and chilled summer berry soup with lillet rosé

the meyer lemon tart [193]
with macerated spring berries, rose water chantilly, and candied buddha's hand

cheeky raspberry tart [196]
with basic berry jam and lavender honey agar-agar gems

pluots baked in muscovado sugar & floral olive oil [198]
with spiced hazelnut-almond mirliton cake, crème fraîche chantilly,
and blackberry & lemon verbena soda

strawberry shortcake [200]
with crème fraîche chantilly and warm strawberry–pinot noir sauce

layered crêpe cake [202]
with orange flower water diplomat cream

layered crêpe cake brulée [204]
with orange flower water diplomat cream, bosc pears roasted in caramel
& indian spices, butterscotch sauce, and pistachio–vietnamese cinnamon brittle

luxe finish [207]
port & peppercorn glazed mission figs, honey baked crispy phyllo squares,
ricotta-mascarpone filling with cognac, candied buddha's hand

dark chocolate soufflé [208]
with three-minute chocolate sauce and burnt caramel ice cream

the sexy chocolate coupe [210]
dark chocolate crémeux, bittersweet flourless chocolate cake, hazelnut spears

double molten chocolate cake [212]
with bing cherries braised in syrah & star anise and tahitian vanilla bean ice cream

that's what i call breakfast [214]
orange-scented waffles with "toffee"; roasted white peaches with olive oil,
lavender honey & sea salt; cherry-vanilla ice cream

We've covered ingredients, recipes, and techniques, but there are two elements above all that are essential for creating alchemy and great desserts. These elements are love and passion.

I am thankful to have found a passion for what I do at such a young age, and now at thirty-three to have the ability to create in our kitchens at Tout Sweet every day with my staff. If as a child I was supported by the first desserts I ate, my mom's cooking, and my mentors; today it is my staff that holds me up to be a better chef. Without them it would be impossible for me to do what I do. Although they come to my kitchen to learn and discover their paths in becoming great pastry chefs, their passion and drive remind me every day why I love this profession and push me to create something different consistently, to never be satisfied with the ordinary.

In the beginning of this book I spoke of my personal definition of "sweet alchemy." It is the combination of a chef's heritage plus their interpretation of a recipe, with a dash of science and technique. The beauty is that we each carry with us a food heritage. I don't want to remove the home cook from this equation. Think back to your favorite childhood meal, the stories that it came with, and the ways that you make it today. My sister Sebnem, also my favorite person in the world, is naturally a good cook. She makes a chestnut rice pilaf, with flavors and techniques from our childhood, that, over the years, has become her own recipe. She is not someone who reads cookbooks or spends relaxing evenings at the stove, and still she has created this kitchen alchemy through her own draw to heartful, scrumptious food memories. Let me put it another way: If my sister can make some kitchen alchemy, anyone can. Truth!

One of the strongest forms of memory that we all carry with us is our food memory. We all must eat to survive, and when survival and pleasure combine, our brains take on a powerful drive to search out the experience again. Sebnem also loves strawberry fraisier cakes, or as she lovingly refers to them, "the strawberry thing." Every year in June I get a call with a request for "my birthday cake." Being a well-trained younger brother, I know that she wants the basic chiffon–pastry cream–chantilly–strawberry torte that we both loved as children. The year that I was grand marshal for the San Francisco Pride parade, I invited her to come celebrate among my friends with me. Her birthday coincided with the festivities, as did the birthday of my co–grand marshal, Olympia Dukakis. I had a lot going on that weekend, so my sous chef made a strawberry fraisier cake for each birthday woman. Here is where food memories are telling: Olympia Dukakis loved her cake, while

my sister, a sibling and an outspoken Turk, took one bite, shot me an accusatory look, and said, "You didn't make this!" As I mentioned before, she is not a culinary genius; she is simply the sister of a chef with a particularly discerning palate when it comes to the desserts of our childhood. My sous chef had used techniques learned outside of my kitchen and created a perfectly delicious cake that did not live up to my sister's expectations. When we bite into something, especially something from our childhood, we expect certain textures, flavors, and scents. We want to be transported to that magical, special place that food memories hold. In professional kitchens, we create systems of checks and balances so that every cake is made the way Chef makes it. That way, when you walk through the pâtisserie doors, you are able to repeat specific food memories over and over again.

Alchemy is the ancient desire to create gold, the standard of perfection, from other earthly materials. The alchemist's goal is almost an impossibility: to transmute lead into gold, to bestow immortality. The very act of cooking is its own form of alchemy, transmuting a series of ingredients into a final product that is more than the sum of its parts. There is a sweet alchemy in the bringing together of separate recipes to create one beautiful combination. In this chapter, I have put together some combinations that I hope will bring out your inner child while tackling your sweetest cravings. The combinations are endless, but these are some of my favorite ways that the recipes can play with one another. If butter and flour, eggs and dairy, sugar and chocolate, fruit and flowers all lift each other up to new heights, then look at the pages that follow as mini chapters in this book.

the luscious raspberry

creamy mascarpone bavarian, citrus-scented almond génoise cake, salty hazelnut & brown sugar crumble, baked berry meringue kisses, organic raspberries

Don't let the dainty preciousness of these parfaits fool you—they are layers of flavor. This combination creates beautiful, complex flavor in one bite. The génoise and Salty Hazelnut & Brown Sugar Crumble bring crunch and a salty, nutty kick, while the creamy, fatty goodness of the mascarpone Bavarian gives your tongue something to look forward to. The fruity, acidic addition of the Baked Berry Meringue Kisses and the raspberries turns everything into a dessert you can be proud of. **YIELD: 10 SERVINGS**

---

1 Citrus-Scented Almond Génoise Cake (page 60)

1 recipe Creamy Mascarpone Bavarian (page 100)

250 g/1 cup Salty Hazelnut & Brown Sugar Crumble (page 46)

100 organic, ripe raspberries

50 Baked Berry Meringue Kisses (page 78)

Use a ring mold or a round cookie cutter to cut ten round disks, 2 in (5 cm) in diameter, from the génoise. Set ten stemless red wineglasses or glass bowls on a baking sheet.

Fit a pastry bag with a plain, round piping tip (no smaller than #3) and use a binder clip to secure the bag shut where it meets the piping tip. Fill the pastry bag with the Bavarian, remove the binder clip, and then pipe a small layer—3 tbsp—into the bottom of each glass. Put a cake disk on top, and then pipe more

Bavarian to cover the cake. This can be done up to 1 day in advance. The cake will absorb some of the moisture from the Bavarian and will become even more delicious.

Just before serving, sprinkle 25 g/1½ tbsp of the crumble evenly on top of the Bavarian in each glass, and place 10 raspberries and 5 meringue kisses among the crumbles. Serve and enjoy.

lavender pavlovas
with lychee, raspberries, and vanilla bean chantilly

This dessert got me my position with Taste Catering in San Francisco, when I was looking to relocate from Las Vegas. I asked one of the owners, MeMe, to tell me flavors she hated in desserts, to which she responded, "You mean flavors I like?" She eventually listed lavender and lychee as two of her least favorites. When I came out to do my tasting with them a few weeks later, I created this little beauty, which combines the robust flavors of rose, lavender, and lychee in a very subtle and playful manner. Once MeMe and the rest of the Taste gang tried these pavlovas, their faces were full of joy, I got the job, and this became a staple on our menu. **YIELD: 10 SERVINGS**

---

10 French Lavender Pavlovas (page 76)

500 g/1 cup Vanilla Bean Chantilly (page 81)

2$^1/_2$ peeled lychee, quartered

10 ripe raspberries, cut in halves

10 Crystallized Organic Rose Petals (page 143)

Place each Pavlova on a plate, a little off center. Fill a deep cup or bowl with hot water (very hot tap water is fine) and set the chantilly next to the hot water. Dip a large soupspoon into the hot water and then immediately skim the spoon along the top of the chantilly to create a quenelle. The heat from the water will cause the chantilly to shine and add elegance to the dish. Place the quenelle of chantilly in the divot of one of the Pavlovas. Wipe the spoon clean and repeat this process until each Pavlova has a quenelle of chantilly on top. If a quenelle is just not your style, place a heavy dollop of chantilly in the center of each Pavlova and move on.

Place 1 quarter of lychee, 2 raspberry halves, and 1 rose petal onto each quenelle of chantilly. Press each bit of garnish gently to set it into the chantilly, but don't squish.

A delicate crumb on the outside and a lovely soft chew on the inside characterize a great Pavlova. To achieve this perfect texture, assemble this dish 30 minutes before you plan to serve it so that the chantilly begins to soften the inside of the meringue and the flavors of the lychee and the raspberry begin to meld with the lavender pavlova. But don't assemble them too far in advance so they don't get too mushy, up to 2 hours is ok. Serve and enjoy.

negroni creamsicle

citrus-scented panna cotta; blood orange, grapefruit & campari gelée; citrus suprêmes; lime zest

A couple of dear friends of mine, Mags and her partner Jill, aside from being fabulous people, are really talented mixologists. One day Mags concocted a Negroni with blood orange vodka and handed it to me as I walked in the door. I was struck by the bitter complexity of flavor, and before the end of the evening I had decided to convert it into a dessert. Where there is great inspiration and great cocktails, creativity comes quickly, and this beauty came to life. This dessert has a lot going for it; it's fairly simple to bring together, can be made for a large group, and can prepared a few days in advance—what's not to love? Make sure you have great, ripe citrus, and I encourage you to sip on a tasty Negroni while you work. **YIELD: 8 SERVINGS**

---

1 recipe Blood Orange, Grapefruit & Campari Gelée (page 125)

1 recipe Citrus-Scented Panna Cotta (page 84)

1 ruby red grapefruit

1 blood orange

1 Valencia orange

Grated zest of 2 limes (see page 110)

At least two hours in advance, or up to 1 day ahead, prepare the gelée and divide among eight stemless wineglasses. Use an egg carton to support the wineglasses at 45-degree angles and allow to set according to the recipe. Prepare the panna cotta and cool to room temperature. Once the gelée has set, remove the glasses from the egg carton and place on the counter. Pour the panna cotta into the wineglasses, filling them to within $1/2$ in (12 mm) of the top, as desired. Return the glasses to the refrigerator for at least 1 hour, or up to 4 hours.

Meanwhile, cut the grapefruit, blood orange, and Valencia orange into suprêmes (see page 113). Just before serving, place one of each of the citrus suprêmes onto each panna cotta. Garnish with lime zest and enjoy.

strawberry-lime sorbet vacherin

with lemongrass poached rhubarb, lemongrass & ginger ice cream, baked berry meringue kisses, and chilled summer berry soup with lillet rosé.

When I presented this dessert on the finale of *Top Chef: Just Desserts,* one of the judges said that it looked pink, frilly, and girly, but when she tasted it, it was complex, deep, and sophisticated. This sort of complexity is what I live for.

YIELD: 8 SERVINGS

---

1 recipe Strawberry-Lime Sorbet (page 126)

½ recipe strained Lemongrass Poached Rhubarb, rhubarb pieces only (page 132)

20 small organic strawberries, halved

40 green pistachios, shelled

24 Baked Berry Meringue Kisses (page 78)

¼ recipe Lemongrass & Ginger Ice Cream (page 96)

¼ recipe Chilled Summer Berry Soup with Lillet Rosé (page 121)

SPECIAL EQUIPMENT:

1 silicone mold with 8 round cavities, or eight 2-in (5-cm) ring molds

---

Remove the sorbet from the freezer and set it in the refrigerator for about 20 minutes to make it easier to work with. Fill the cavities of the mold with sorbet completely, packing it to be sure there are no air pockets, and then use a small offset spatula to smooth the tops. Once filled, immediately transfer the mold to the freezer to set until very hard, at least 2 hours. Ideally, this should be done 1 day in advance. The more the sorbet is set and frozen, the cleaner the lines of the molded sorbet. When you are ready to unmold, gently push up on the mold from the bottom to free the sorbet. Place the molded sorbets onto a baking sheet lined with parchment paper, wrap with plastic wrap, and store the entire sheet in the freezer until ready to use. Do this ahead of time so that you don't have to struggle to unmold the delicate sorbet.

CONTINUED . . .

When ready to serve, set out eight shallow soup bowls, place 15 to 20 pieces of the rhubarb around the edge of each bowl, divide the strawberry halves throughout each ring of rhubarb, and then scatter the pistachios among the berries and rhubarb to create circles of fruit and nuts. Place 3 meringue kisses in the very center of the bowl. From the bottom of each sorbet round, scoop out a heaping 1 tbsp, creating a cavity so there is room for the meringue kisses to nestle underneath. Put one molded sorbet round over the meringue kisses in the center of each bowl. Place a small scoop of the ice cream directly on top of the sorbet. Finally, use a pitcher or a ladle to gently pour $2\frac{1}{2}$ tbsp of the chilled soup onto the fruit and nuts. Make sure not to pour the soup on top of the ice cream or sorbet, to keep the sorbet and ice cream intact. Serve and enjoy.

the meyer lemon tart
with macerated spring berries, rose water chantilly, and candied buddha's hand

A true test of a great baker and/or pastry chef is not in developing outrageously complicated desserts. Instead, it is in perfecting the simplest of preparations. We've all had lemon tarts, but a well-prepared tart demonstrates true craftsmanship. If you take the time and put in the proper love, you will find that a GBD (golden brown and delicious) crisp tart shell combined with a very well-prepared lemon custard is nothing short of perfection.

Meyer lemons are a cross between lemons and Mandarin oranges, and they harness the beautiful qualities of both—tart yet still sweet and fragrant. In this recipe, the flower essences of the rose-flavored chantilly cool off the tart sensation on your palate as the burst of tangy sweetness from the macerated berries brings a depth of red fruit to the dish. **YIELD: 10 SERVINGS**

---

340 g/2 cups cherries

500 g/2 cups strawberries

340 g/2 cups raspberries

1 recipe Raspberry & Red Verjus Sauce (page 115)

Ten 3-in (7.5-cm) baked Sweet Almond Tart Shells (page 57)

¹/₂ recipe Meyer Lemon Curd (page 127)

Grated zest of 1 lime (see page 110)

Grated zest of 1 lemon (see page 110)

Grated zest of 1 orange (see page 110)

10 pieces Candied Buddha's Hand (page 129)

3¹/₃ cups (790 ml) Rose Water Chantilly (page 82)

Pit and halve the cherries, hull and halve the strawberries, and leave the raspberries whole. Place into a large bowl and toss gently; pour the verjus sauce over the fruit and use a rubber spatula to fold so that the fruit is covered in sauce. Allow to macerate for at least 10 minutes.

Set out your baked tart shells and use a rubber spatula to stir and break up the lemon curd. Fit a pastry bag with a #3 plain piping tip, use a binder clip to secure the bag closed at the opening to the tip, and then fill the bag with the lemon curd. Remove the binder clip and

CONTINUED . . .

pipe the lemon curd into the tart shells to just fill them. Spoon a small amount of the fruit mixture onto the center of each filled tart and sprinkle with some of the zest of each citrus.

Pile the Candied Buddha's Hand pieces on a small plate on the side, along with a bowl of the chantilly, and pass them at the table when serving, so that your guests can top the individual tarts to their taste.

Sweet Note: To use Candied Buddha's Hand as a plate garnish, or as a tart or cake decoration, drain slices on a cooling rack set over a rimmed baking sheet or baking pan for 2 or 3 hours, pat dry, toss in granulated sugar, and let dry overnight. Use whole or cut into shapes.

cheeky raspberry tart
with basic berry jam and lavender honey agar-agar gems

One woman who has been a great inspiration to me throughout my entire life is the singer Björk. The way in which she creates music, harnessing the elements of the classics and then turning them upside down and inside out, is unconventional and absolutely beautiful. To purists her music may be obnoxious, but there is no denying her talent. To those daring enough to experience the exquisite, Björk is truly a gift. I created this dessert using an approach similar to the one she takes when creating music. The raspberry tart is a classic French preparation, but here I turn it upside down and inside out. The sweet aroma of the vanilla accents the acidity of the jam-filled raspberries, while the lusciousness of the pastry cream acts as the chorus, holding the entire thing together—and why not sprinkle the entire tart with translucent, honey-sweetened agar-agar gems? Seriously, this is not what you think it is—it's better. **YIELD: ONE 10-IN (25-CM) TART**

One 10-in (25-cm) baked Sweet Almond Tart Shell (page 57)

¼ recipe Basic Berry Jam (page 119)

½ recipe Vanilla Bean Pastry Cream (page 88)

500 g to 1 kg/2 to 4 cups raspberries

Thirty ⅛-in (4-mm) squares Lavender Honey Agar-Agar Gems (page 28)

Set the baked tart shell in the center of a serving platter. Fit one pastry bag with a #1 plain tip and fill it with the jam. Fit a second pastry bag with a #3 plain tip and fill it with the pastry cream. Pipe the pastry cream into the tart shell, then smooth it out with a small offset spatula. Reserve 15 firm, ripe raspberries. Starting at the outside edge, meticulously line the raspberries in a circle, with the tips faceup. Tuck the next circle of raspberries into the first and continue until the tart is full of raspberries, interlocked with one another. Take the 15 reserved raspberries and pipe jam into each one, until plump and filled with jam. Sit each filled berry, jam-side up, into the berry-lined tart, scattered throughout as though they are flirting with you and your guests. Tuck the agar-agar gems within the crevices of berries so they shine like little jeweled rocks throughout the red raspberries. Slice it up and enjoy.

pluots baked in muscovado sugar & floral olive oil

with spiced hazelnut-almond mirliton cake, crème fraîche chantilly, and blackberry & lemon verbena soda

If the Luscious Raspberry takes the feminine lead in this book, then this dessert would certainly star in the masculine role. The flavors in this dessert are masculine yet refined and deeply complex, like a great, handcrafted cologne. Roasting the pluots accentuates their tartness and their explosive, juicy qualities; and the sprinkling of Caribbean muscovado sugar brings in a certain depth and maturity. All this harmonizes with the roasted, nutty, and spiced flavors of the mirliton cake. If you serve this seasonally with the Blackberry & Lemon Verbena Soda, you can imagine yourself in the 1950s chatting with Mark Twain about Paris. **YIELD: 3 OR 4 SERVINGS**

Spiced Hazelnut-Almond Mirliton Cake (page 101)

½ recipe Crème Fraîche Chantilly (page 82)

½ recipe Pluots Baked in Muscovado Sugar & Floral Olive Oil (page 136), quartered

1 recipe Blackberry & Lemon Verbena Soda (page 122)

Cut the cake into small cubes. Coat one half of the inside of your serving bowls with a smear of chantilly. Place two or three of the pluot pieces in the bowls, cut-side up. Top with the cake cubes. Serve accompanied by glasses of Blackberry & Lemon Verbena Soda.

strawberry shortcake

with crème fraîche chantilly and warm strawberry–pinot noir sauce

This is one of the first desserts I learned to prepare as a young pastry cook at the age of nineteen. I can still recall how challenging it was for me to get the crumb on the shortcake biscuit as perfect as that achieved by my first pastry chef, Noah Butter. Perhaps his last name gave him a certain magic. The deep strawberry flavor of the sauce, combined with the richness of the Pinot Noir, creates a perfect sangria flavor that plays off of the whipped crème fraîche. Even now, this seems like a simple preparation when I'm making it, but I'm still surprised by my love of the flavors. **YIELD: 8 SERVINGS**

---

8 Crème Fraîche Shortcakes (page 54)

1 kg/4 cups medium strawberries

2 recipes Warm Strawberry–Pinot Noir Sauce (page 116)

1 recipe Crème Fraîche Chantilly (page 82)

Powdered sugar for dusting

Preheat the oven to 350°F (180°C). Use a serrated knife to gently slice the shortcakes through the middle, taking care to not break them; they will be delicate and crumbly. Prepare the strawberries by cutting off the green hulls and, if large, cutting them in half lengthwise. Line a baking sheet with parchment paper and set the shortcakes, cut-sides down, on the parchment. Toast in the oven for 6 to 7 minutes. In a small skillet over medium heat, bring the sauce to a boil. Set out eight shallow bowls.

Let the shortcakes cool for 2 minutes, until they are warm to the touch. Place the bottom half of a shortcake in the center of each bowl and put a generous dollop of chantilly in the center. Line the shortcake with strawberries standing up around the chantilly and gently push them into the cream to secure them. The chantilly should meet up with the strawberries and come up over the tops of the berries a little bit. Just before serving, sprinkle powdered sugar over the shortcake tops while they are still on the baking sheet and then place a top over the chantilly on each shortcake. Use a pitcher or ladle to pour 1/2 cup (100 ml) of the warm sauce around the edge of the bowl. Serve and enjoy. If you find that your shortcakes start to soak up the pinot noir sauce, don't fret—this is a gateway to heaven!

layered crêpe cake
with orange flower water diplomat cream

A very classic crêpe cake, known as a *crepage* in Italy, is a staple in most French pâtisseries. What makes this timeless classic so delicious is the precise 23 layers—12 layers of paper-thin crêpes and 11 layers of diplomat cream—flirting with your fork as it slides down each meticulously placed, consecutive layer, not to mention the textural contrast between the chewy and the creamy. Most classical preparations use orange zest to give depth to the diplomat cream, but I like to use a bit of orange flower water for a fragrant, Mediterranean flair. **YIELD: ONE 10-IN (25-CM) CRÊPE CAKE, ABOUT 12 SERVINGS**

Twelve 10-in (25-cm) Paper-Thin Crêpes (page 48)

1 recipe Orange Flower Water Diplomat Cream (page 90)

This preparation is helped along by a 12-in (30-cm) cake board and a cake decorating turntable. Place the cake board onto the turntable and use a large binder clip to secure it in place. Set a crêpe in the center of the board, and use a #6 scoop to measure ¾ cup (180 ml) of diplomat cream onto the crêpe. Hold an offset spatula at an angle in the center of the cream and, with your other hand, turn the turntable, spreading the diplomat cream into an even layer until it just barely reaches the edge of the crêpe.

Repeat 11 more times, and finish with a crêpe on top. You will have 12 layers of crêpe and 11 layers of diplomat cream, with a crêpe on the top and the bottom. Make sure to bring the diplomat cream all the way out to the edges of the crêpes, or the finished cake won't look as inviting.

Refrigerate for 2 hours before serving to ensure that the layers set. If preparing the night before, cover with plastic wrap once set.

layered crêpe cake brulée

with orange flower water diplomat cream, bosc pears roasted in caramel & indian spices, butterscotch sauce, and pistachio—vietnamese cinnamon brittle

Each one of these components stands alone as a classic preparation of a dessert, but this combination of spice, aroma, and texture brings them to a more contemporary place. As a pastry chef cooking to please people, I find one challenge to be that some want modern and innovative while others want classic and comforting. The beauty of this dessert is that it hits notes that are both modern and classic. From the colors to the flavors, it is a true celebration of fall in all its glory; the sweet, spicy flavors of the roasted pears and the brittle play with the delicate, creamy flavors of the meticulously layered crêpe cake, while the sultry flavors of the brown sugar in the butterscotch sauce, as well as the caramelized crunch of the brûlée, hold it all together from top to bottom. **YIELD: 12 SERVINGS**

Layered Crêpe Cake with Orange Flower Water Diplomat Cream (page 202)

6 Bosc Pears Roasted in Caramel & Indian Spices (page 140)

1 recipe Pistachio—Vietnamese Cinnamon Brittle (page 34), unbroken

Powdered sugar for brûlée topping

1 cup (240 ml) Butterscotch Sauce (page 32)

Preheat the oven to 250°F (120°C). Use a very sharp knife to cut the crêpe cake into 12 slices; after each cut, clean the knife with a damp towel to keep your sliced edges clean and sharp.

Cut the pears in half lengthwise. Use a melon baller to scoop out the seeds, if desired, and then halve the pears again, yielding 24 quarters. Lay the quarters in the roasting pan used to roast the pears and place the pan in the oven

CONTINUED . . .

to keep warm until ready to serve (the pears can be in the oven for up to 30 minutes without becoming overcooked). Break the pistachio brittle into thirty-six 1- to 2-in (2.5- to 5-cm) pieces.

Immediately before serving, sprinkle each cake slice generously with powdered sugar and use a kitchen torch to cook the sugar. It will caramelize and bubble up. Torch it until the top of the slice is a beautiful, deep golden brown and smells of cooking sugar.

Set out 12 dinner plates. Place 1 tbsp butterscotch on the lower half of each plate, and use the back of a spoon to make a swoosh on the plate. Put a cake slice in the top right corner of the plate, at an angle with the back facing you. Diagonally across from the cake, and near the center of the butterscotch swoosh, lean two pear quarters against each other. Garnish with three pieces of pistachio brittle and serve.

luxe finish

port & peppercorn glazed mission figs, honey baked crispy phyllo squares, ricotta-mascarpone filling with cognac, candied buddha's hand

Think of this as a luxurious crossover of a cheese plate and a summer dessert; a tango between the luscious flavors of mascarpone, ricotta, and citrus paired with the sultry flavors of figs basted in port. The crispy phyllo sheets bring the two together and add crunch. Whether you serve this with wine or cocktails or as the end to a luxurious dinner, the flavors are sure to please the palate. Invite your guest to pile the figs, cream, and candied citrus in any order—they will enjoy! **YIELD: 10 SERVINGS**

---

1 recipe Port & Peppercorn Glazed Mission Figs (page 134)

2 recipes Honey Baked Crispy Phyllo Squares (page 62)

1 recipe Ricotta-Mascarpone Filling with Cognac (page 86)

½ cup Candied Buddha's Hand (page 129), cut into strips, or candied orange

---

On a clean counter, lay out three to five (depending on size) large serving platters, decorative cutting boards, or food-safe slates. Divide the figs and phyllo squares between the platters, arranging them attractively and leaving room between them for the filling.

Use a piping bag fitted with a wide, flat tip, or an intact piping bag cut at a 45-degree angle to give the same effect, to pipe a decorative swirl of the ricotta filling in the center of each serving platter. Alternatively, use a large spoon dipped in hot water to place three dollops of the filling in a diagonal line along the center of each platter.

Finish the platters by sprinkling with the strips of Buddha's hand and drizzling some of the pan juices from the roasted figs on the fruit.

dark chocolate soufflé

with three-minute chocolate sauce and burnt caramel ice cream

This combination has been tested time and time again. You can't go wrong with dark chocolate and burnt caramel. The intensity of the caramel and the bittersweet chocolate matches well with the extreme contrast of the steaming hot soufflé and the chill of the ice cream. I encourage you to pour the chocolate sauce tableside into the soufflé, because it creates a pool of goodness that you'll find your guests delightedly digging into. **YIELD: 5 SERVINGS**

½ recipe Dark Chocolate Soufflé batter (see page 172)

1 cup (240 ml) Three-Minute Chocolate Sauce (page 178)

250 g/1 cup Salty Hazelnut & Brown Sugar Crumbles (page 46)

1 cup (240 ml) Burnt Caramel Ice Cream (page 98)

Prepare five individual soufflés, without baking, up to 6 hours in advance. Preheat the oven to 375°F (190°C). Gently place the soufflés in the center of the oven and bake for 7 to 10 minutes. While the soufflés are baking, warm up the chocolate sauce and stir to emulsify it so that it is warm and ready to go when the soufflés come out of the oven. Place 2 tbsp of the hazelnut crumble on the left side of each plate.

After 7 minutes, check on your soufflés. They should have risen at least 1½ in (4 cm) above the tops of the ramekins. A perfectly baked soufflé will be just barely soft in the middle, so that there is a dime-size spot in the center that is just a little bit darker than the rest of the soufflé. If the soufflés are not ready when you check them, bake for another 2 to 3 minutes.

Scoop a generous amount of ice cream on top of the crumble. When the soufflés are done, place one on each plate, opposite the ice cream. At tableside, push a serving spoon directly down into the center of each soufflé and then rotate it 90 degrees to create a well in the center. Pour about 2 tbsp chocolate sauce onto the spoon so that it slides into the soufflé. Serve immediately and enjoy.

the sexy chocolate coupe

dark chocolate crémeux, bittersweet flourless chocolate cake, hazelnut spears

My business partner MeMe giggles girlishly every time I refer to a dessert as "sexy," but in truth I think all dessert should have some sex appeal. When we brought this together in the kitchen, I knew we had a great flavor combination, but I felt stumped by the visuals, until MeMe suggested adding the hazelnut spears. Her idea brought the dessert from sleepy to sexy in one simple step. **YIELD: 10 SERVINGS**

50 g/10 tsp cocoa nibs

Bittersweet Flourless Chocolate Cake (page 170)

1 recipe Dark Chocolate Crémeux (page 161)

1 recipe Vanilla Bean Chantilly (page 81)

10 Hazelnut Spears (page 37)

10 dark chocolate half-moon decorations (see page 152)

1 sheet of gold leaf (optional)

In a medium sauté pan, cook the cocoa nibs over low heat for 2 to 3 minutes, until a distinct nutty scent develops. Remove from the heat and set aside.

Use a 2-in (5-cm) ring mold or round cookie cutter to cut ten disks out of the chocolate cake.

Set out ten stemless wineglasses or decorative parfait glasses. Fit a pastry bag with a plain, #3 piping tip, and use a binder clip to secure the bag closed where it meets the piping tip. Fill the bag with the *crémeux*, remove the binder clip, and pipe 2 tbsp into each glass, covering the bottom. Put the cake rounds on top of the *crémeux*, and then pipe another 2 tbsp of *crémeux* to cover the cake. Use a tablespoon to put a large dollop of chantilly on top of the *crémeux*, and then sprinkle each with 5 g/1 tsp roasted cocoa nibs. Gently place 1 hazelnut spear, pointed-side up, into the chantilly; use a twisting motion so that it sits securely in the chantilly. Put a chocolate half-moon decoration on the edge of each glass. If desired, put a small bit of gold leaf onto each chocolate half-moon for a bit more glitz. Serve and enjoy.

double molten chocolate cake
with bing cherries braised in syrah & star anise and tahitian vanilla bean ice cream

Chocolate and cherries are star-crossed lovers. They each bring out the best in the other: good chocolate has a natural fruity tang, and perfectly ripe bing cherries have a deep, rich, cocoa flavor. I believe this cake is like a really sexy romance. It's deep, rich, tasty, and at times messy. But the messy is what makes it delicious. The secret to plating this dessert is timing. Keep your ice cream cool right up until it is time to serve, and bake the cakes at the last possible moment. The results, like true love, will be magical.

YIELD: 10 SERVINGS

---

1 recipe Double Molten Chocolate Cake batter (see page 168)

2¹/₂ cups (600 ml) Tahitian Vanilla Bean Ice Cream (page 92)

1 recipe Bing Cherries Braised in Syrah & Star Anise (page 130)

20 to 30 pistachios, halved

Prepare the cake batter. The batter can be made and held in the refrigerator up to 5 days in advance. If you do pre-mix the batter, pull it out and set it on the counter at least 1 hour ahead of baking.

When the batter is ready to be baked, remove the ice cream from the freezer and place it in the refrigerator for 10 to 15 minutes. This will allow the ice cream to come to a firm but creamy consistency.

While the ice cream is softening, bake the cakes according to the recipe directions.

Scoop the ice cream into each serving dish, just a bit off-center. Then use an offset spatula to scrape a flat surface across the top. This will make it look like a small, turned-out pint of ice cream.

Place each warm cake in the center of a serving dish. Spoon 8 to 10 braised cherry halves around the cakes, as well as some of the braising liquid. Sprinkle the pistachio halves around the cherries and serve.

that's what i call breakfast

orange-scented waffles with "toffee"; roasted white peaches with olive oil, lavender honey & sea salt; cherry-vanilla ice cream

This is one of those magical dishes that has a contrast of temperatures and textures in all the right ways. The rich, juicy peaches bring sweet acidity, while their heat balances the cold of the ice cream. It all comes together on a bed of waffles that are crunchy on the outside and fluffy on the inside. If you are fortunate enough to have wild fennel flowers growing nearby, pick some and sprinkle them on top of this dish just before serving. Their anisette flavor will add an unexpected surprise, and their star-shaped prettiness is downright adorable. **YIELD: 2 SERVINGS**

½ recipe Roasted White Peaches with Olive Oil, Lavender Honey & Sea Salt (page 138)

2 Orange-Scented Waffles with "Toffee" (page 65)

1 cup (240 ml) Cherry-Vanilla Ice Cream (page 94)

Fennel flowers for garnish (optional)

Prepare the roasted peach by cutting each half into three slices, so you have six crescent-shaped peach slices. Prepare the waffles according to the recipe. When I prepare this dessert, I like to make the waffles organically misshapen so that they are not perfectly round or square. They will be best enjoyed fresh off the waffle iron. Cut each waffle in half diagonally.

Set out two plates and on each plate place one waffle half and lean the second half against it so it stands up. Tuck three peach slices around the waffles on each plate. Place a scoop of the ice cream on top. If the ice cream begins to melt, fear not; it will create a wonderful sauce for the warm peaches and waffles. Garnish with fennel flowers, if desired, and serve.

sources

The following is a list of sources for equipment and ingredients used in this book.

KING ARTHUR FLOUR
www.kingarthurflour.com

Baking and pastry tools and equipment, specialty flours, gluten-free flour mix, vanilla beans, vanilla bean paste, chocolate.

SURFAS CULINARY DISTRICT
www.culinarydistrict.com

Baking and pastry tools and equipment, bakeware, molds, agar-agar powder, vanilla beans, vanilla bean paste, verjus.

L'EPICERIE
www.lepicerie.com

Fine spices, extracts, flavorings, and hard-to-find ingredients, including agar-agar, glucose syrup, vanilla bean paste, Vietnamese cinammon, and verjus.

PENZEYS
www.penzeys.com

Spices and herbs, including vanilla beans, star anise, Vietnamese cinnamon, and softstick cinnamon.

index

Page numbers in italics indicate where a recipe is used as a component of another recipe.